MADE TO SHINE

a girls only devotional

MADE TO SHINE

a girls only devotional

Snowfall Press
Printed in the United States of America

ISBN Paperback 978-0-9910598-0-5
ISBN eBook 978-0-9910598-1-2

Cover Design and Interior Layout Design: Sarah O'Neal | evecustomartwork.com
Cover Photo Courtesy of Lightstockphoto.com/Baryden Heath

To order this book please visit:
www.sonflowerz.com

DEDICATION

This devotional is dedicated to the Hopner Girls, the Dennis sisters, and Bethany. God dearly loves each of you, and our prayer is that you will always surrender your whole heart to Jesus. He alone can guard your heart and give it true life. You are some of the many girls who compelled us to finish this book by your questions, your emails, and being part of our lives. Thank you!

~ MANY THANKS ~

To our Mom and Dad for cheering us on, being examples of Christ's light and showing us the way. Our husbands for the amazing love and support we needed to write our best. Our editor Margot Starbuck for keeping us smiling and making us better writers. Pam Gibbs for your enthusiasm and for being a fantastic sounding board. Susie Shellenberger for encouraging us to keep writing and reaching girls. Vicki Courtney, thank you for your friendship and your example. Paige Green, Amy Cato and Michelle Hicks - much of our inspiration for this book came from *You & Your Girl*. It was an incredible journey! Laura Tucker, thank you for your expertise. Sarah O'Neal, you added the ever-so-important icing on the cake. We loved working with you!

CONTENTS

This is For You i
Our Playlists iii

Light Source

1 :: Your Canvas 1
2 :: Up Close and Personal 5
3 :: The Promise Keeper 9
4 :: Love Letters 13
5 :: I Heard God Speak 17
6 :: Flip the Switch 21
7 :: Borrowed 25

Unveiled Brilliance

8 :: President's Daughter 31
9 :: Who He Says I Am 35
10 :: #2601 39
11 :: Irreplaceable 43
12 :: Beauty Lessons 47
13 :: Miss Understood 51

Sacred Radiance

14 :: Single? Me? 57
15 :: The Ring 61
16 :: The Kiss 65
17 :: Wearing White 69
18 :: A Thousand Bouquets 75
19 :: What About True Love? 81
20 :: The Dream Life 85

Glow in the Dark

21 :: Drama Queen 91
22 :: Fight Like a Girl 95
23 :: Sister vs. Sister 101
24 :: 70x7 105
25 :: Defeating Depression 111
26 :: Battlegrounds 117

In the Limelight

27 :: The Incline 125
28 :: First Response 129
29 :: Courageous Beauty 135
30 :: Between the Songs 139
31 :: Cooking Up Compassion 143
32 :: Let's Get Together 149
33 :: Made to Shine 155

THIS IS FOR YOU

So you want to be noticed? Don't we all. We want to be the girl that everyone turns to see strutting her stuff down the halls, the one with that contagious smile and perfectly timed jokes—that girl. We resonate with the idea of shining so deeply. Even if you are quick to say you like to stay in the crowd, unnoticed, I bet there is a hint of curiosity inside, wondering, "What would it be like to stand out?"

Who could you be if you really did shine?

But the qualifications to being a standout chick aren't quite clear. Do we have to be popular or the prom queen? Do we need natural charm or a line of boyfriends at our door? Not exactly.

Everything hinges on who you are shining for. Is it for you? For fame? I shine for God. He's the One who created us for it. "You're here to be the light, bringing out the God-colors in the world," Jesus said. "God is not a secret to be kept. We're going public with this, as public as a city on a hill. If I make you light-bearers, you don't think I'm going to hide you under a bucket, do you? I'm putting you on a light stand. Now that I've put you there on a hilltop, on a light stand—shine! Keep open house; be generous with your lives. By opening up to others, you'll prompt people to open up with God, this generous Father in heaven" (Matthew 5:14-16, The Message). There's boldness about light, a sheer defiance against the dark. So it is with those who shine.

I wrote a song when I was 14—my first song (and it was rough)—called "Use Me." I never sing this song now, but when Becca and I wrote this book "Made To Shine," I suddenly remembered the lyrics. You'll see why:

To shine on this earth is to be noticed for what you live by
I cry to shine forth, for my Savior, who gives me life.
Lord, shine me in the dark.

Woven into my first song were the themes of shining, purpose, ambition, and Jesus.

From that first time I picked up the pencil, my songwriting sparked a boundless love to play guitar and sing. Although I wasn't a great musician, and I didn't carry around an American Idol voice, "Use Me" and other songs like it gave me the drive to start a band. They were the reason I went on the road, too. It was all because of a message.

We shine because of His light within us. It has nothing to do with our outside appearance or the stuff we have!

A real relationship with Jesus is the beginning of shining; without a connection to Him, shining is impossible. And Jesus sends His Spirit to guide us through this life as His light-bearers. Without the Holy Spirit we are helplessly searching around in the dark trying to find the light switch! We can't actively shine without God's help. And so commences the challenge to welcome the Source of light, Jesus Christ and His Spirit, to flow through you each day.

Come on a journey with Becca and me. Take each day, each page of this book as a challenge to find out what the best life can look like. It's not easy, but completely worth it. As your sisters in Christ, we dare you to go for it!

We're with you.

Elissa

The Sonflowerz

OUR PLAYLISTS

From our iPods, we've selected some of our favorite songs for you each day. In our opinion, this is awesome music you should own! You may already have these songs, or maybe you will download the playlist everyday from iTunes.

At the end of reading each day, take a listen. Or, if you're like Becca, you'll probably turn up thetunes as you read the devo. Either way, by the end of the book, you'll have the most rockin' music library ever.

HERE IS A HINT

HINT: Can't buy the tunes, but want to hear 'em? Google "Grooveshark"—this is a fantastic site that pays royalties to the artists for online streaming!

I LITERALLY GASPED OUT LOUD when I saw this story on the news. The alarm was raised in room 17 of the art museum after a gallery assistant spotted a man spraying two paintings with an aerosol can. Brilliant works from 1633, completely covered in red spray paint! Though these paintings had survived centuries, a trigger-happy fool destroyed them in a moment.

All of us carry a canvas of God in our mind's eye, a painting of His character. For Hailey, it was her parents' divorce that altered her canvas. The day her dad walked out, never to return, put a deep smear across her understanding of who God really is. Margaret lost her house in a fire when she was eight and her big sister ran away from home when she was ten. These girl's experiences created unforgettable smudges disfiguring their view of God. "Will God leave me too?" they thought.

We all desperately need to find the true picture of God.

What words would you use to describe God? If He were painted on a canvas, what would His *eyes* say to you?

DESCRIBE~

Spraying over God's image through lies, pain, and letdowns, humans keep adding to the canvas. By a stroke, a spray, a mark with their own cans of aerosol, they hide the one-of-a-kind piece. Then it's hung in a public gallery and the masses make a verdict: He is angry, disappointed, or uninterested. All the while, the true face of God is buried beneath, unseen.

But God is real, and *He* should have the final say on who He really is.

TODAY'S PLAYLIST

What Love Means :: Everfound
Come To Me :: Jamie Grace
Til I Got To Know You :: Sanctus Real

Here's the truth: We see God when we see Jesus. He is the untarnished picture of God, on display! Jesus revealed to the world how infinitely God loves us.

The restoration work on our damaged canvas is long overdue! Friends, it's time to allow the steady hand of God's Son, Jesus Christ, to chip away at the drips and stains. You may very well find that the true picture of

> The aim of art is to represent not the outward appearance of things, but their *inward* significance.
> ~Aristotle

God is more beautiful than you could have imagined.

As a middle-school kid, I experienced God's love for the first time at youth camp. The atmosphere stirred me as I watched my friends worship and connect with God. Something powerful took place. Suddenly I handed over the brush as Jesus painted the picture of God in my heart. I was captured. As my sister and I began the journey of becoming The Sonflowerz, singing together and writing songs, it became our mission from day one to share this truth with other girls: "We look at this Son and see the God who cannot be seen. We look at this Son and see God's original purpose in everything created" (Colossians 1:15, The Message).

> *By a stroke, a spray, a mark*
> *with their own cans of aerosol,*
> *they hide the one-of-a-kind piece.*

REFLECTION & ACTION

1. Read Ephesians 3:16–19. Ask Jesus to reveal to you the true character of God.

2. In 1 Corinthians 13:12 it says, "*now we only see a reflection . . .* " What do you think that means? (**HINT**: If you don't have a Bible in front of you, you can always search the Scripture reference on the Internet.)

PER·SPEC·TIVE
[per-spek-tiv]
the proper or accurate point of view or the ability to see it; objectivity

Until Heaven, we only know what we imagine God to be, when really only He knows how He should be defined

LOVE Letters

COLOSSIANS 2:9
JOHN 1:1–5 "In the beginning... Word was God"

light source

Up Close & Personal

EVER SEEN STORYTELLING from a "felt board"? These are my earliest, most classic memories of Sunday school. My teacher, Mrs. Bowling, used little felt characters to act out Bible stories. It may sound sorta hokey if your leaders are using iPads and TVs, but when you're little, let's just say it was crazy awesome. Somehow this (literally!) fuzzy interpretation of Jesus, Mary, Joseph, angels, and donkeys made the stories come alive.

In those stories, I realized that people walked for miles to hear Jesus teach. Imagine that! They were sincerely drawn to Him, no matter their background or lifestyle. Jesus made God more real—not only to the people He encountered, but to me and my friends right there in Sunday school. From the words He spoke to the way He loved downright messed-up people, we saw that God truly cares about us. Now, my understanding of Jesus became much larger than a felt board cutout. He isn't just someone I read about, He is living in my heart. It's truly amazing. How did this change happen within me?

Jesus isn't just someone I read about

I remember picking up my guitar for the first

time. Attempting to play those first songs was so frustrating. I couldn't get anything down for months. But then I began to disconnect from the struggle and simply sang out my thoughts to God as I played a simple chord. When I was playing, God's Holy Spirit, His near presence that we

TODAY'S PLAYLIST

My Heart Is Alive :: The Sonflowerz
No Ordinary Love :: TobyMac
All I Need :: Bethany Dillon

can't see with our eyes, brought me comfort, peace, and joy. It was as if a soft breeze swept over me. And, right there, I experienced what it is to know God in my heart.

Jesus gave His life when He died on the cross because He loves us. When I think of a love that big, I can hardly grasp it! He knew that our sin, the ways we missed the mark God set for us everyday, had separated us from God. Jesus could have prevented His death, but instead He chose to die in our place to pay the price for our wrongs. He was willing to do anything it took so that we wouldn't be distanced from Him.

Jesus was willing to do anything it took so that we wouldn't be distanced from Him.

anything!!

The Bible is like a love letter written to us from God. And here's a verse that unearths something amazing: "Because of His great love for us, God, who is rich in mercy, made us alive in Christ even when we were dead in transgressions – it is by grace you have been saved" (Ephesians 2:4–5). Think of that! When we were least likely to have a second chance, Jesus made it possible.

As I got to know Him the way I know my family and friends, I fell in love with Jesus. It didn't feel like work, either, because I wanted to know Him! The way I spent time with Jesus, discovering a personal relationship with Him, was with simple prayers and by digging into the New Testament. But my favorite expression was always singing my songs to Him.

You can't have a true relationship with someone just by knowing him or her from a distance; you have to connect in a real way. God wants this kind of relationship with you. He wants to make Himself known to you each day, whether you find Him through music or Scripture or a prayer while riding your bike. Each day may be different. The key is taking time to connect with Him.

REFLECTION & ACTION

1. Is Jesus more to you than stories you've heard? (continued on next page)

List all the things Jesus is to you:

2. Talk to God about your desire to connect with Him in a real way, and to experience the love He has for you.

CON·NEC·TION
[kuh-nek-shuhn]
part, link, bond,
relationship,
circle of friends

JOHN 3:16

light source

ONE CRUSHED GIRL WROTE to me, "I don't understand. My boyfriend said he would always love me. Now he laughs at me in front of his friends."

A promise is defined as a declaration or assurance that one will do a certain thing or guarantees that a particular thing will happen. And promises come at us from all directions.

Political candidates vow to save the planet once they are in charge. TV commercials try to convince us to buy carpet cleaners, diet pills, and anti-aging serums that never work. Boyfriends make plenty of promises, too.

The world is full of promise makers and promise breakers. But what ever happened to promise keepers?

Think about the reliability of the morning sun or how the stars never fail to fill the sky at the end of each day (even on the cloudy days!). Picture the ocean's strong tide and the moon's consistent glow. All of these point to our Promise Keeper.

I love this passage: "Don't put your confidence

in powerful people; there is no help for you there. When they breathe their last, they return to the earth, and all their plans die with them. But joyful are those who have

TODAY'S PLAYLIST

Promises :: Jared Anderson
He is With Us :: Love And The Outcome
Find You On My Knees :: Kari Jobe

the God of Israel as their helper, whose hope is in the Lord their God. He made heaven and earth, the sea, and everything in them. He keeps every promise forever" (Psalm 146:3–6, NLT).

Remember Jesus' prayer in the Garden of Gethsemane, the night before the cross? He was faithful to choose to go to the cross for us, even though He knew it would be extremely painful. Faithfulness isn't just something God *has*; it's who He *is*. Jesus Christ is the same yesterday today and forever (see Hebrews 13:8).

But, betrayals come at us from every angle—the friend who sides with the popular crowd instead of you, the guy who shoves you away, the parent who leaves without saying goodbye. With this kind of wounding, it's easy to build

Faithfulness isn't just something God has;

{it's who He is.}

skepticism towards everyone around us. We may even begin to doubt God, too. But His love for us never changes despite the unfaithfulness of others and even our own! The rough times we experience are perfect opportunities for our trust in God to grow stronger. He is trustworthy, even if no one else is.

For the girl who had been disrespected by her ex-boyfriend, I replied to her letter with my favorite passage about God: "Though the mountains be shaken and the hills be removed, yet my unfailing love for you will not be shaken nor my covenant of peace be removed" (Isaiah 54:10). A covenant is a heartfelt agreement, a vow—and God is speaking it to us!

Is there a situation in your life, good or bad, that has influenced your view of God, the Promise Keeper?

JOT IT DOWN

The most marvelous promise of our lives is that Jesus is coming back for us. See how He is described: "I saw heaven standing open and there before me was a white horse, whose rider is called *Faithful* and *True*" (Revelation 19:11-14, emphasis mine).

No one else can keep a promise like God. He won't leave your side when you've been disappointed by others. He is the ultimate Promise Keeper.

REFLECTION & ACTION

1. Ask God to reveal and to heal the hurtful experiences that might prevent you from trusting Him.

FAITH·FUL·NESS
[feyth-fuh-ness]
true to one's word,
reliable, dependable
trusted

2. Read Psalm 37 and write down each promise from God to you in that chapter.

REVELATION 21:4
PSALM 34:4

light source

FOR A WHILE I HAD been feeling like reading my Bible was a chore. Just one more thing on my daily to-do list. I wore that badge of self-achievement proudly, having read the Bible cover-to-cover many times. *I know what it says,* I thought, *and God can always remind me of Scripture when I need Him to.* It's not as if I never read it. I just wasn't in it every day.

Then a crazy thing happened to me. I left for a trip to lead worship for a retreat. I felt like the woman speaking that weekend was speaking just to me. (Has that ever happened to you?)

She began by telling her story. As a victim of rape in college, she had found herself desperate for God to rescue her from daunting fears that plagued her every day.

How did she climb out of this dark place? It was the Word of God that soothed her and restored her. She read Hebrews 4:12, "For the Word of God is alive and active. Sharper than any double-edged sword, it penetrates even to

How would you feel if you didn't eat anything for days?

dividing soul and spirit, joints and marrow; it judges the thoughts and attitudes of the heart."

As I listened, I was in a dark place of sorts. For weeks, my voice had been frail, so frail that I could barely sing. It was scary for me because a line-up of important trips

You Know Me :: Bethel Music
Wonderful :: Desperation Band
Run To You :: Kari Jobe

was on my calendar. I changed my diet in hopes that this would help me. On top of that, I was taking medicines and vitamins, and praying like crazy to get my voice back.

What God spoke to me through this woman's testimony was revolutionary. Yeah, I was missing something in my diet—God's Word! She read this: "Man does not live on bread alone but on every word that comes from the mouth of the Lord" (Deuteronomy 8:3).

So if I need more than bread to live, and I'm not *eating* God's Word every day, then I must be malnourished!

How would you feel if you didn't eat anything for days? Well, that's what I was doing to my spirit by not reading the Bible regularly.

For what felt like the first time, I knew that reading the Bible wasn't a duty. It was a necessity for life and for my healing.

Back then, if I could have rated my daily Bible intake

on a scale from one to ten (one being the lowest), it would definitely have been around a three. I saw my spiritual life looking like a malnourished child needing food.

How would you describe your "Bible intake" right now?

When you read the Bible, you will discover God's marvelous pursuit of mankind. How He created us for the purpose of being in a love-filled relationship with Him, and how people chose other gods besides Him. Page after page tell of how God still pursued us with love.

Jesus is the ultimate pinnacle of God's love chasing us down. We encounter what that love is like in the Scriptures. When we read the Bible, we begin see ourselves in the pages. Words jump out to us, speaking right into our need.

On the flight home from the retreat, I set a plan to carve out space every day to open up a chapter in the Bible. In the weeks that followed, as my voice was slowly restored, I discovered the power of His Word to change me from the inside out.

REFLECTION & ACTION

1. Find a Bible translation that speaks your language. There are outstanding study Bibles

with maps, pictures, and all kinds of explanations to illuminate what is said. (Becca is into the New Living Translation right now, but I often read the NIV as well as The Message.)

2. For one month, team up with a friend and read through the book of John in the Bible. Keep each other accountable to reading some daily. And be sure to discuss the topics you read. (Before you go for it, remember that missing a day of reading isn't cause for a guilt-trip. Over time you'll develop the habit.)

PSALM 33:4
PSALM 119:89

ONE OF THE MOST defining moments of my life occurred when I heard God speak to me for the first time. My very best friends had just turned their backs on me. I was a lonely, heart-broken twelve-year-old. Crying myself to sleep, I prayed for God to give me good friends I could count on.

And right there, in my lowest moment, I heard Him whisper in my heart, "I will bring you friends, and the first one will be named Amanda." I considered this strange, and I immediately doubted that these thoughts could be God, but I waited to see. A couple weeks later a new girl arrived in my sixth grade class. Her name was, astoundingly, Amanda. Some may call it coincidence, but my little heart was overwhelmed by God's careful attention to my simple prayers.

Shortly after, my family moved across the country. *Well, that was convenient,* I thought. *Now I have to start over finding friends?* Saying goodbye to my hometown was an all-time low. I got in our moving van trying to hide my apprehension. But when we arrived, I practically stepped out of that van to meet my first friend, who, of course, was also named Amanda. This "Amanda" thing was pretty cool. Just another way God was reeling me in to His love.

TODAY'S PLAYLIST

Sound of Your Voice :: Third Day
Stop and Listen :: Bethany Dillon
Edge of My Seat :: The Sonflowerz

How do we hear God's voice? He speaks to us through the Bible, and His Spirit has a direct line to our hearts. When have you heard God speak to you?

RECORD IT:

You can probably guess that there are things that keep us from hearing God speak. Willingly giving into sin is a big hindrance. Sometimes we have to do a 180, turning away from other things in order to turn to God. Being too busy to spend time with God is another major roadblock. He needs our attention, time, and our fullest trust.

People talk about having a soft heart towards God so we can learn to hear His voice. A soft heart has no walls up and no limitation on what God can say. What if God says something that requires you to change or bend to His design? A hard

God invites us into conversation every day!

heart would hold up a stop sign telling God not to come any closer. But, by nature, God always longs to be in closer communication with us.

The Guinness World Record for the loudest burp is over 100 decibels, executed by a man from the UK.

John's gospel confirms that Jesus, who knows us intimately, also intends to be known by us. "I am the Good Shepherd. I know my own sheep and my own sheep know me. In the same way, the Father knows me and I know the Father . . . (My sheep) recognize my voice" (John 10:14, NIV).

When God spoke to me about Amanda, it was a life-changing moment. But it caused me to realize that He had been speaking to me long before that time, in much more subtle ways. A beautiful sunset, my mom's hugs, a pick-me-up through Scripture, or the thrill of answered prayer. God invites us into conversation every day.

Now you know. You *can* hear the voice of God.

REFLECTION & ACTION

1. Are your prayers two-way conversations? Take a minute to ask God to help you hear His voice. It may not be instantaneous, but you can start by learning to listen for Him as you pray.

2. Listening to Scripture and to God's voice speaking to your heart, what might God be saying to you today?

CON·VER·SA·TION
[kon-ver-sey-shuh]
informal interchange of thoughts and information

PSALM 23
JOHN 10:1-14

light source

day 6

FLIP the SWITCH

by elissa

HAVE YOU EVER SEEN the reality TV show called "Buried Alive"? It's about people who have overloaded their houses with junk. So much junk that they can't get around from room to room. On the show, it's not uncommon for the home to be stacked to the ceiling with unopened Christmas presents and boxes from online shopping orders.

Ready with masks and gloves, the cleaning team goes in. These miracle workers uncover black mold and insects rummaging through trash.

And people *live* in this!

As I watched one episode unfold, the homeowner was extremely emotional, even indignant, as volunteers helped sift through the waist-high clutter. She didn't want to see the ugly mess and deal with it. For her, keeping things as they were was security.

A false kind of security.

We often feel safe in familiar surroundings, even if our surroundings are harmful piles of trash! If our hearts are anything like a house, then there are rooms that need attention.

God wired the whole house with electricity by giving you the Holy Spirit.

Fear. Sin. Regret. Guilt. Pain. What room in your heart's house might contain some of these leftovers from your past?

"Buried Alive" got me thinking about my own life. Are there dark and dusty rooms inside of me filled with boxes and garbage? Maybe I've cracked open the door once or twice and thought, *This is too much to handle. I'll deal with it some other time.*

Love Walked In :: The Sonflowerz
Endless Light :: Hillsong Live
Marvelous Light :: Christy Nockels

But even if I could find enough courage to start uncovering the clutter, at the end of the day, I can't fix up my own heart. The mess still exists.

Trying to get my heart right on my own is like cleaning a wrecked house in the dark! This search for righteousness—or a clean heart—can be endless.

When you became God's child, He wired the whole house with electricity by giving you the Holy Spirit. As a result, the cleanup can really begin!

Girl, you and I need some light! What would happen if you flipped the switch on in every room of your internal house? The Holy Spirit is the light who comes in with healing and restoration.

It's not about putting things in order by yourself, but

> **Faith** is the strength by which a shattered world shall emerge into the light.
> **~Helen Keller**

instead letting God have His way in you. His intention is to do all the heavy lifting, but we have to choose to leave the light on—no matter how painful the sifting and removal of garbage may be.

Don't get caught buried alive! What our hearts look like on the inside really matters. When we offer our mess, God accepts us and turns the whole situation around.

REFLECTION & ACTION

1. The dilemma isn't whether or not you have a messy room; we *all* do. Have you flipped the switch to expose it to the Light? Ask the Holy Spirit, our Counselor, to help you shine light in every dark place of fear, sin, regret, guilt, or pain.

2. Find an older mentor or a parent to pray with you about this area of your life where you have committed to see change. Write down a name in the space below.

LIGHT
[lahyt]
something that makes things visible, illumination source

3. **Remember:** The cleanup is directed and accomplished by God, in His grace, His power, and His timing. Turn your ear to His voice during the process.

1 THESSALONIANS 5:23-24
1 JOHN 1:7

light source

day 7

borrowed

by elissa

IN THE SUMMER OF 2010, I was happily engaged and waiting for a fantastic wedding day. I had no idea that my fiancé, Chad, was busy preparing for our new life together by selling off his beloved piano. When he told me the piano was gone, I gasped. (But, this sacrificial choice paid for our honeymoon.)

Once we were married, I was shocked by my husband's enthusiastic ability to let go of things. As newlyweds we had loads of empty space in our house. Not a lot of stuff to our name, and yet I would find Chad giving away computers, guitar gear, and books. I could barely contain my knee-jerk reaction to chase after the folks he was generous to and take back the things he gave away.

I wonder how many times I've sung these words in a church service to God: "It all belongs to You."

David praises God in 1 Chronicles 29:11, "Yours, Lord, is the greatness and the power and the glory and the majesty and the splendor, for *everything in heaven and earth is Yours*" (emphasis mine).

But if everything is God's, does that mean nothing is mine?

Everything in heaven and earth belongs to God!

I'm overwhelmed by the urge to preserve what I have, maintain control, and protect what's in my possession. This just highlights my need to know God better. He's not out there to squash my joy in life; He's here to provide for me like a good Father. Simultaneously, He is a Dad who wants us to be free of self-centered, self-satisfying, greedy ways.

TODAY'S PLAYLIST

The Stand :: Hillsong United
Everything is Yours :: Audrey Assad
After Your Heart :: Phil Wickham

Take a look at the things you've collected over the years: from the priceless heirlooms to the so-called junk. A stockpile of Christmas gifts, dusty Barbies, or heaps of clothes. Do any of these things hold onto you? Do the things you own, own you?

Give yourself a rating from one to ten, one being "I love giving stuff away" and ten being, "I'm always afraid God will ask me to give something away." ___________

Whatever your answer, you are not alone. I admit, it's difficult to let go. But the narrow, often challenging path of a Christ-follower includes living open-handed before God, with a heart like clay, moldable in His hands (like silly putty). Your heart doesn't have to

attach to the stuff you have; instead, you can find your treasure in God. He is enough.

I'm in process of believing all of God's promises for me. He guarantees us some pretty amazing things. But while I'm on this journey, I pray that my heart would rest in His love and not be wrapped up in my stuff. I'm fully aware that "where my treasure is, there *my heart* will be also" (Matthew 6:21 paraphrased).

Shortly after my husband gave away his piano, a marvelous thing occurred. A family friend told us he needed a place to store his *gorgeous grand piano*. While our friend was overseas for years with the military, we became the proud stewards of this exceptional instrument. What a gift from God!

I'm overwhelmed by the urge to preserve what I have, maintain control, and protect what's in my possession.

Today I saw this beautiful piano in my house, paused, and prayed, "God, You are in control of my desires, and everything I have is Yours. It's all borrowed from You. Thank You for each gift. And help me to remain willing to give just like You do."

REFLECTION & ACTION

1. Are you living with tight fists or open hands?

2. Read Romans 8:32 and journal what it means to you.

TREA·SURE
[trezh-er]
valuable things, to regard or treat as precious

3. How crazy would it be to take the word "mine" out of our vocabulary? Try it for a day!

LUKE 6:38
PSALM 145:13

my thoughts

BRIL·LIANCE
[bril-yuh ns]
splendor, elegance
or magnificence

president's daughter

EVER WONDER WHY no one in the Bible has a last name? You have Paul, David, Esther, and Mary, but where's that last name? The best we get is "Saul son of Kish"! No reference to a Mr. Saul McDonald.

When I was beginning the fourth grade, I was transferred to Tomas Rivera Elementary. The school was so new I could still smell the fresh paint and carpet when I walked in for the first time.

Our neighborhood had been assigned to this new district, and many parents were not thrilled about their kids being forced to move schools. My parents were in the same boat, so they decided to get involved. Even though his life was already busy running a business, my dad offered to start the school's first Parent Teacher Association.

The PTA kickoff meeting was held in the school auditorium. I noticed a table with nametag stickers and black Sharpies. Grabbing a nametag for myself, I wrote, "Daughter of Don Leander—PTA President." Apparently, I didn't care if people knew my first name or not! I was the daughter of *the president!*

There is an identity out there greater than any family name.

Slapping the nametag on my shirt, I left the table confident that my dad was the president. Every word that came out of my 9-year-old mouth, even how I treated everyone in the room, was a direct result of this confidence.

Now That I Am Yours :: The Sonflowerz
Father :: Hillsong United
You Invite Me In :: Meredith Andrews

Who are you? What would you write on a nametag? Your answer to this question has the ability to change everything.

There is an identity out there greater than any family name. The name each one of us was born with can limit and define us. When you think about a family name, your thoughts are turned toward the *past* and what people *did*. You reason, *This is me. I can never be more*. Hold up. Before you limit yourself in this way, remember that you are in God's family now, and that means focusing on the present, not the past. "Praise God for the privilege of being called by His name" (1 Peter 4:16).

Take a second to fill in this blank with a list of characteristics that first come to mind:

I AM:

i've heard it said

We have a chance to be born again, to connect to our eternal purpose.

Are any of the characteristics you wrote down like your own parents? My dad and I are similar in a lot of ways. (Just ask my mom!) Yet my Heavenly Father is the one who truly defines me. We can simply fill in the blank with, "I am His."

There are a plethora of labels that we give ourselves. But God wants to strip away every label until we see ourselves complete as a daughter of God.

Some days I forget the privilege of being called "His." I'm trying to be someone I'm not or I get bogged down with popularity. My need to belong to something worthwhile is strong. But Jesus has put an end to this longing – we belong to Him.

I have a suspicion about the missing last names in the Bible. Perhaps God wants to make this statement to us:

> *First and foremost, you are My daughter. Don't think too much about your identity elsewhere; I want you to know that your identity is wrapped up in Me.*

My excitement about being called a president's daughter that night eventually awakened me to my true identity. I am the King's daughter. "...to all who did receive him, to those who believed in his name, he gave the right to become children of God" (John 1:12).

REFLECTION & ACTION

1. What aspect of your family's name and identity has boxed you in?

2. Why do you or don't you feel like a part of God's family?

3. Ask God to reveal your born-again status as His daughter, so that you live out this belief today. "I am HIS."

1 JOHN 3:1
ISAIAH 41:9-10

unveiled brilliance

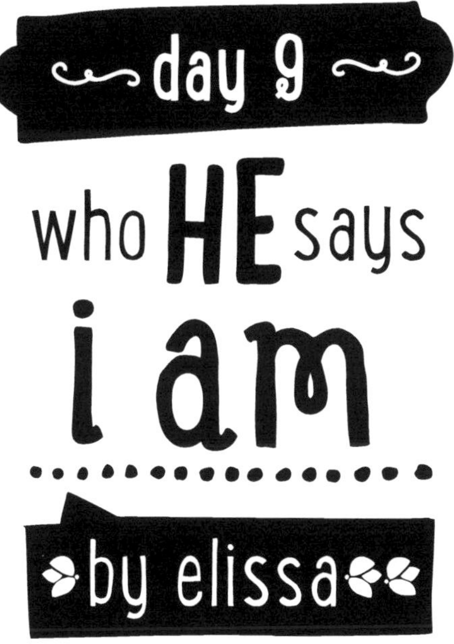

MY MOM HAS CARRIED a piece of worn out paper in her Bible for years. It's a list of scriptures declaring who we are in Christ. When I faced difficult, teary-eyed moments in my life, she would whip out this paper and begin reading it to me. "You are a child of God" (Romans 8:16); "you are a new creation in Christ" (2 Corinthians 5:17); "you are forgiven" (Colo. 1:13–14); "you are complete in Christ" (Colossians 2:10). My mom told me that she prayed these things over me, too. Photocopied a bazillion times, the paper is now in my own Bible, in my suitcase, and by my bed.

Wherever I am, I need to be reminded of who I am because of Jesus. But, sometimes I am guilty of forgetting who God says I am.

During the recording of one of our CDs, I found myself wondering if my singing ability was strong enough or even worth recording. I'm often given opportunities to perform, but then I question if I have what it takes to get on those stages.

Wrap yourself in the thought that God calls you His daughter.

It's only when I sit down with the words that God speaks about me that all of these negative thoughts disappear!

When you think about the great lengths God went to in order to send His Word to us, how does that make you feel?

TODAY'S PLAYLIST

Dearly Loved :: The Sonflowerz
Beautiful :: MercyMe
In the Beginning :: Bethany Dillon

Insecurity can't hang around long in the heart of a child of God. We are not left to struggle through life alone. We are not given tasks too big to handle (even when we feel overwhelmed). We walk day by day with the Creator of the world! With Him, all things are possible and we are completely taken care of. Wrap yourself in the thought that God calls you *His* daughter. He treasures you as His own.

His words, not ours, have the final say.

Believe this: You are the adored girl of God (John 3:16). You are His chosen servant (John 15:16) and you are given gifts from His heart in order to glorify Him (Ephesians

1:3). You are victorious in any challenge that may come (Revelation 21:7). You are more than a conqueror (Romans 8:37) and delivered from darkness (Colossians 1:13). You are holy and without blame before Him in Christ (1 Peter 1:16). The list doesn't stop there, but I'm running out of paper!

The key is to agree with who God says you are. If this is hard to do, stick a verse on your mirror and tell it to yourself every morning until it settles in!

His words, not ours, have the final say. Even when we forget and make mistakes, we can look up and remember again, *I am a dearly loved daughter of God.* Nothing can change this reality and every day we have a new chance to live it.

REFLECTION & ACTION

1. Which one of the identities listed in the devo did you need to hear today?

Wherever I am, I need to be reminded of who I am because of Jesus.

2. How will you choose to walk out your real, God-given identity?

COLOSSIANS 3:12

THE NUMBER JUMPED OUT from the page. Katelyn had found out a year earlier that she was adopted, and she had begun to search for more information on her birth parents. But when the certified mail finally came, she was stunned to read the paperwork. Specifically, she was shocked to discover that there was no record that her birth mother had given her a name. The lack of personal attention her birth mother gave her—not even enough to name her before giving her away—felt unbelievable. According to official record, she was "number 2601," like a passcode, or a house number. Below it she read, "Father's name: unknown."

For Katelyn, the revelation of "2601" translated into "unwanted." She felt herself slip into despair. Those words had power to discourage and dampen her soul.

Perhaps you've read something about yourself, or have a memory of something that happened in your past, and your heart has sunk into a hopeless spiral because of it.

Maybe the voice is even closer than a person or a document. Perhaps it's your own voice. As you look into the mirror you hear it. The moment you mess up anything, it condemns: *Ugly. Stupid. Accident-prone. Failure.*

The reality is, we've all believed lies about ourselves. The words fester within us, mocking us every time we come up short or feel unworthy.

TODAY'S PLAYLIST

Little Lies :: The Sonflowerz
Beautiful Things :: Michael Gungor
Suitcases :: Dara McLean

But, negative words spoken to you in your past don't have to define you today or shape your future. God has spoken the deepest truth about who you are throughout the pages of the Scriptures. And when held up to the light of what God says about you, the lies simply don't stand. It's a matter of choosing who you'll believe.

Even better than spending hours learning how to hula-hoop, play Risk, or touch your tongue to your nose,

God has spoken the deepest truth about who you are throughout the pages of the Scriptures.

The average person thinks **1,200** unconscious negative words per minute.

is practicing how to think the truth about yourself! Look up each Scripture below and write what it says about your true identity:

Ephesians 1:4 — I am ____________________
Malachi 3:17 — I am God's____________________
John 1:12 — I am God's ____________________
1 John 4:10 — I am ____________________

As tears unloaded down Katelyn's face, out of desperation she flipped open her Bible on the coffee table. Feeling a nudge she knew came from God, Katelyn opened to the page of Isaiah 49:1: "The Lord called me before my birth; from within the womb He called me by name" (NLT).

Like a warm drink on a bitter cold night, the verse comforted her. It exposed the lie even as the report began to settle in. Unwanted? No. She was *chosen*.

Who will you choose to believe? Katelyn could have elected to believe that because of her birth parents' decision not to name her or keep her, she was unlovable, unwanted, and unworthy. The course of her entire life would have changed. But because she threw those papers away, picked up her Bible and let the words of her Father in Heaven go deep into the crevices of her heart, she was transformed into a fearless girl of God.

She believed God. And that changed everything.

REFLECTION & ACTION

1. Sticky notes are my favorite. Use them to write down a Scripture you looked up and post them where they're visible, as you get ready in the mornings.

2. **Change your speech!** Your body, soul, and spirit listen to every word that's spoken, by you and others, and most of the time, they *become* what they hear. Consider what you speak about yourself each day, and ask God to help you change your speech to reflect truth.

JOHN 15:9
JOHN 8:32

unveiled brilliance

irreplaceable

RUMMAGING THROUGH AN unused dresser, I found it. The vibrant oranges, blues, and pinks hadn't faded much. I pulled it out from the dresser and stared at the lace, admiring the homemade stitching on each layer.

With its vintage patterns, I instantly fell in love with my mom's old blouse. She wore it as a British hippy in the 1970s. The lady who sold it to her said it had been made from an antique bed spread!

My first chance to wear it on stage was at a summer festival near the Great Lakes. A mom and her daughter greeted me afterwards. They were eager to know where I shop. I smiled and told her the story of my well-traveled top. Later I grabbed a hot dog, loaded it with mustard, and thought, "I better eat this carefully. I'll never find another shirt like this!"

When was the last time you discovered something vintage, one-of-a-kind. . . something *irreplaceable?* Perhaps it's hung up in your closet or has a special place in your room.

DESCRIBE IT HERE

God considers us His irreplaceable treasures. How do I know this? Each one of us is so precious to God that He was willing to give what He loved most. Imagine what it must have felt like for God to give away His only Son on our behalf. It's impossible to fully grasp how deep the Father's love is for each one of us.

TODAY'S PLAYLIST

10,000 Reasons :: Matt Redman
Your Love Never Fails :: Newsboys
More Than I Think I Am :: The Sonflowerz

And God carefully thought through every detail when He created you. The writer of Psalm 139 says, "How precious to me are your thoughts, God! How vast is the sum of them! Were I to count them, they would outnumber the grains of sand." We get another glimpse of God's thoughts about us from Ephesians 2:10, "For we are God's *masterpiece.* He has created us anew in Christ Jesus, so we can do the good things He planned for us long ago" (NLT, emphasis mine).

With its vintage patterns, I instantly fell in love with my mom's old blouse.

There is no second copy of you—even if you were born a twin! You are significant to God's plan for humanity - not average or ordinary.

> We were each chosen for a particular, cosmically important task that can be done by *no one else.*

God specifically designed your qualities, looks, and style. He gifted you with purpose like no one else. What's one way you can thank God for how He's created you? By being you! Acting like other people, or comparing yourself to others, is not what God had in mind for you. You owe it to yourself to *be* yourself!

When I wore that vintage blouse this summer, I was clothed in something irreplaceable. Unique. Only one was ever made. How amazing! Now I can understand how my Father sees me.

Yes, me. Yes, you.

REFLECTION & ACTION

1. For me, the shirt is a reminder of how irreplaceable I am. What object in your room or closet symbolizes this for you? Find a way to display it!

2. Extend this truth to someone else. Today, share this with a friend who may be forgetting she's irreplaceable too.

You owe it to yourself to be yourself!

EPHESIANS 1:4-6

beauty LESSONS

GROWING UP, I NEVER REALLY liked my hair. I envied those girls in the magazines who had shiny, smooth locks. Because I couldn't compete with what they sported, I decided to hide my frizzy hair in a ponytail. To make matters worse, I was unsuccessful in all my attempts to cover up my terrible acne! All I could see in photos were my flaws.

Anyone relate?

The truth is all of us can think of something about our bodies we aren't thrilled about. I didn't like my hair and acne-prone skin. Someone else doesn't like her nose. Another girl doesn't like her hips.

It's so easy to get stuck thinking destructively. We see beauty in people, just not in ourselves.

Why? Did God make a mistake? Before you begin to think so, check out this passage in the book of Psalms: "For you created my inmost being; you knit me together in my mother's womb. I praise you because I am fearfully and

Her endless striving to be a perfect weight, get noticed by guys, and compare favorably with other models brought her to her knees.

wonderfully made; your works are wonderful, I know that full well" (Psalm 139:13–14).

The way I felt about my so-called imperfections made me wonder how I could see myself the way God sees me. There are still flaws I mentally list when I look in the

TODAY'S PLAYLIST

You Captured Me :: The Sonflowerz
More Beautiful You :: Jonny Diaz
Through My Father's Eyes :: Holly Starr

mirror. But now I take that list to God in prayer, along with all the stuff I feel insecure about, and it becomes my own modern-day psalm.

Does the image in the mirror consume your thoughts?

True beauty isn't surface-level. But deciphering what exactly true beauty is becomes a tricky thing when Facebook selfies and fashion magazines cause us to focus on external appearances.

It's thoughts like these that trigger comparisons and compromise our *inner* beauty when we try to impersonate the "top model." Genuine inner beauty is difficult to uncover on Instagram and Facebook, don't you agree?

Peter wrote this in a letter that hits hard even today: "Don't be concerned about the outward beauty of fancy hairstyles, expensive jewelry, or beautiful clothes. You should clothe yourselves instead with the beauty that comes from within, the unfading beauty of a gentle and

People who worry about their hair all the time frankly, are *boring*.
~Barbara Bush

quiet spirit, which is so precious to God" (1 Peter 3:3–4, NLT).

Former supermodel Jennifer Strickland has a powerful story about how God changed the way she thinks about herself. She wasn't the "perfect picture," though on the outside you might have thought so. Always unhappy with herself, even as a model, Jennifer attempted to fill the emptiness and loneliness she felt, but she never could. Her endless striving to be a perfect weight (which doesn't exist), get noticed by guys, and compare favorably with other models brought her to her knees. She left the modeling world and has never turned back. "God has given me a purpose," she says. "To share His love, to tell the stories of my life that display so powerfully the beauty that God sees in the heart of every woman."

Genuine inner beauty is difficult to uncover on Instagram and Facebook.

Here's a true beauty secret I've discovered: Knowing Jesus more and more unveils a stunning brilliance from the inside of you. He will transform the way you see yourself when you glimpse how radiant you look to Him! That knowledge will fill every empty place, the kind Jennifer felt and the kind I've felt. With His love and acceptance you will shine with God-given beauty from the inside out.

REFLECTION & ACTION

1. Describe someone you know who is beautiful on the inside.

2. How much do you worry over your appearance? How could this keep you from connecting with Jesus?

PSALM 34:5
PROVERBS 31:30

miss understood

RECENTLY I WAS AT RUDY'S—my favorite restaurant for good BBQ. While standing in line, trying to decide between peach cobbler or banana pudding, a family in front of us began to debate. Loudly. I couldn't help but notice a teen girl carrying a massive diaper bag—for her mom—with two younger siblings running in circles around her.

It happened like clockwork. The four-year-old swung back her leg and wacked her older sister full force in the shin. The sibling winced in pain and gave her sister a slap. Like falling dominoes, the baby in the mother's arms began to cry. And the four-year-old began to whine.

The mom suddenly took notice and began to yell and curse at the oldest sister. The teenager was to blame, in the mother's eyes. At this point, the dad looked at them and shouted, "That's it! I'm done with this!" as he stormed out of the restaurant. It was like a siren had gone off—everyone crying. The mom shouted at the teen, "Now you've ruined everything! He's never coming back and it's all your fault!"

Blamed. Rejected. Accused.

Have you ever felt like you were in court and couldn't plead your case before the verdict was made?

TODAY'S PLAYLIST

Oceans :: Hillsong United
Whom Shall I Fear :: Chris Tomlin
Come To Me :: Jamie Grace

After I left Rudy's, I felt remarkably grieved for this family . . . especially the girl, carrying the weight of her family on her shoulders (literally). I wonder how many of you can relate to her?

We aren't meant to carry burdens alone.

There is another person who was often misjudged. He lived an extraordinary life revealing to people the mysteries of God. It was common to find Him sharing a meal and conversation with the misfits and outcasts. When He would leave a room, people were left scratching their heads. "Who was that?" they thought, "and what was He saying?"

This man is Jesus. He ultimately died the death of a criminal, even though He was proven innocent in every way.

Here's a description of Jesus from the book of Isaiah: "Surely he took up our pain and bore our suffering, yet we considered him punished by God, stricken by him, and afflicted. But he was pierced for our transgressions, he was crushed for our iniquities; the punishment that brought us peace was on him, and by his wounds we are healed" (Isaiah 53:4–5).

The punishment that brought us peace was on Him? Here's a Man who can understand a heavy burden. And yet, we find Him saying, "Get away with me and you'll recover your life. I'll show you how to take a real rest. Walk with me and work with me—watch how I do it. Learn the unforced rhythms of grace. I won't lay anything heavy or ill-fitting on you. Keep company with me and you'll learn to live freely and lightly" (Matthew 11:29–30, The Message).

If you're linking arms with Jesus, things aren't going to be perfect, but you'll always make it to the other side. He gets you. He knows the burden you're lugging around.

With Him, you will make it through anything.

We aren't meant to carry burdens alone.

REFLECTION & ACTION

1. Write about a day when you felt misunderstood.

UN·DER·STOOD
[uhn-der-stuhd]
to be thoroughly familiar with

2. Spend a few minutes talking with God about that day, right now.

3. Read 2 Corinthians 4:17–18.

PSALM 121

my thoughts

SA·CRED
[sey-krid]
connected with God or dedicated to a religious purpose and so deserving reverence

I ONCE MADE A RADICAL CHOICE to give up dating altogether. It was right at the outset of my high school career, when all of my friends were pairing off.

I set out to carve another path.

You're probably asking, "Did she have a dating phobia or hard time getting someone to ask her out?" Thankfully, no. I didn't want to spend high school calling the shots. I was ready to jump into the unknown, and let God handle my love story.

The word "waiting" is a huge, daunting word when you're single. But waiting is about God having His way, not my emotionally-driven, sappy heart.

Honestly, what kind of ideas does the word "waiting" trigger in your mind? **JOT IT DOWN**

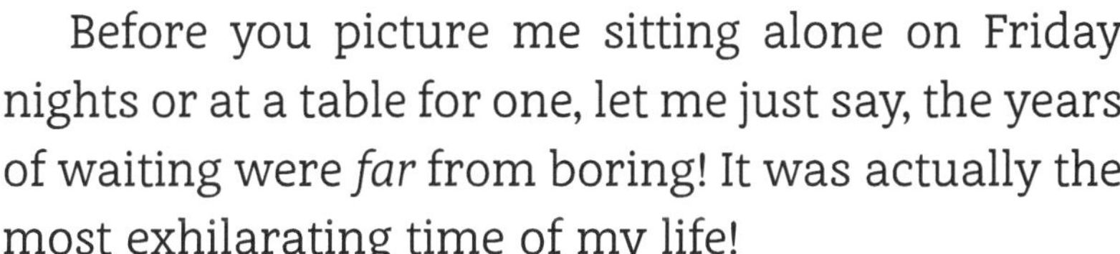

Before you picture me sitting alone on Friday nights or at a table for one, let me just say, the years of waiting were *far* from boring! It was actually the most exhilarating time of my life!

Snowboarding trips, late nights hanging out

with my best girl friends, writing songs, and traveling consumed any free time I had.

But, as great as those things were, the most incredible part was how my relationship with God flourished. He gave me such confidence to be who I was made to be. I

TODAY'S PLAYLIST

Let Go :: Holly Starr
Average Girl :: BarlowGirl
Always Reign :: The Sonflowerz

saw a clearer picture of God's calling on my life and how I could serve Him through music. Singleness went from being lame to the best thing that could ever happen to me.

What was true for the ancient songwriter, King David, is also true for us: "Take delight in the LORD, and he will give you the desires of your heart. Commit your way to the Lord; trust in Him . . . Be still before the Lord and wait patiently for Him . . ." (Psalm 37:4–7).

When those four years of high school were up, I asked God to guard my heart from falling for just any guy. I still needed to give Him full authority to direct my path,

Singleness went from being lame to the best thing that could ever happen to me.

especially now that I was open to dating. I continued to hang on His every word, both the whispers of His heart and the truth found in the Bible, as I navigated through singleness.

And my journey wasn't done alone. I connected to a group of Christ-followers who prayed for me and encouraged me. My parents were also a faithful sounding board.

Driven by true abandon to God, I went forward in seeking His best for my life. I knew that the right man for me would be a complement to my calling. To my surprise, my future husband, Chad, was also serving God in music when I met him. (Amazing, right?)

God has all the details of our lives in His hands. What a relief! My job wasn't to find a husband, but to follow God with all of my heart.

REFLECTION & ACTION

1. How do you spend your time waiting? Would you say your waiting is marked by peace or by anxiety? Explain.

2. Read Proverbs 3:5–6.

3. Write a prayer to God about your desires, hopes, and frustrations with singleness.

WAIT·ING
[wey-ting]
pause, interval
delay

LOVE Letters

PSALM 40
LAMENTATIONS 3:22-26

day 15

the RING!

by elissa

EVERY GIRL HAS A THING OR TWO TO SAY about the wedding ring she wants. Even my minimal input to my husband's pick was precise, but it was my grandma who really impacted my wedding ring choice.

She gave me my first "real" ring. It was a small 14k gold band with a heart in the center, given to her as a purity ring from her father when she was a teen. The significance was huge to me. Grandma had cancer when she gave me the ring, and knew she didn't have much time left. Her instruction was to wear the ring as a reminder to keep myself pure and wait for my husband.

I was young then, but it didn't matter. I knew exactly what she meant.

A few years later, another pivotal moment. Grandma's ring became too fragile to wear and Dad bought me a new one.

That same day in my journal I wrote a prayer to God: "I give You my life, every day to serve and honor You. I give You my heart, my love, my body to worship You." Later I wrote, "I will not be the one fulfilling

A whole heart, unfettered and with zero regrets, is just the beginning.

my own purposes in my life, it will be God fulfilling His purposes for me."

In the most beautiful handwriting I could muster, I entered into my journal Psalm 138:8: "The Lord will fulfill His purpose for me; Your steadfast love, O Lord, endures forever" (ESV).

As I've grown to know God better, I have seen that His plan for me is undeniably good. He desires that I would

All I Want Is You :: Phil Wickham
Offering My Life :: The Sonflowerz
He Said :: Group 1 Crew

be free from everything that hinders me from knowing Him and experiencing His best.

I'm convinced that purity is not about fighting impulses as much as it is about fulfillment. Who is fulfilling your life? Are you chasing down every opportunity to feel loved, like someone trying to catch the wind?

As girls, it's easy to be caught in this fanciful quest for love. When each of us comes to a crossroad, will we choose to hand over our longing to the only One who can fulfill us?

God's love has no boundaries. He can satisfy our hearts like no one else.

So how do you attain purity in your life?

By trying to grab fulfillment *everywhere* we find it *nowhere.*
–Elisabeth Elliot

Saying yes to purity is the first step. You can be sure God's grace will come alongside you to help you do it. Matthew 5:6 gives us this promise: "Blessed are those who hunger and thirst for righteousness, for *they will be filled*" (emphasis mine).

Let me invite you to see purity as the splendid gift that it is, so attractive, so otherworldly. A whole heart, unfettered and with zero regrets, is just the beginning.

On your wedding night, your purity will be a profound treasure to your husband. It places your marriage on a foundation of trust and commitment like nothing else can.

When my close friend Molly got engaged, it caused her to look back at the times in her life when she wasn't living for Christ. Some moments were hard to swallow. She expressed the sorrow of giving away her virginity early on and worked hard to erase thoughts of being with other guys.

With bewilderment, she asked me, "Why didn't my father protect me and warn me about what I was doing?" Molly's dad was a hands-off kind of guy. It made me realize the terrific gift that my father was to me when he handed me that lovely gold band and asked me, "Will you take a stand for purity, Elissa?"

Friend, if no one else has called you to this, let me be the first. *Will you commit to a no-regrets life of purity?*

My husband placed a sparkling diamond ring on my finger when he proposed. That diamond was the very same one my grandmother had worn in her wedding band all her life. I see her diamond every day. Her legacy of full-on commitment to Christ is the kind of thing I want to be remembered for, too.

REFLECTION & ACTION

1. Write down your own vow of purity to God.

2. Read 1 Corinthians 6:18–20.

3. Who is one family member or person in your life that you will tell about your Vow to Purity?

HEBREWS 12:1-2

sacred radiance

WHEN I WOKE UP, God prompted me with a thought and I knew He was speaking to me. As I was barely opening my eyes to the sunlight in my room, He asked me something surprising—"Will you commit to waiting until your wedding day for your first kiss?"

What? I was baffled.

I had promised God that I would be a virgin until I was married, but this sounded extreme. I wanted to just roll over and forget about it, but I couldn't. So I pulled out my journal and began to write. "Okay, God, what do you mean by this?" (Crazy, but this is how God and I work!)

A kiss is just a kiss. Right? I had never dated before. I figured I would decide what seemed right when that time came. Apparently God was posing the question to me now.

I sat there, fully awakened, searching my heart. I pondered whether I was up for this kind of commitment. Recorded in my journal is this uneasy prayer: "Jesus, I want to go a step further and commit this to You." And now I was in conversation

I want you to trust Me in a whole new way.

with God. (Unbelievable!) He spoke again to my heart, "I want you to trust Me in a whole new way. I want to show you that I am your greatest treasure."

On a scale of 1-10, how much do you feel like you trust God with your love life? (1 being not the slightest bit, 10 being "All the way!") _________

Fast-forward eight years. Then enters Chad, the love of my life, and we have just launched into the world of

TODAY'S PLAYLIST

All I Am :: Phil Wickham
Take Heart :: The City Harmonic
God's Great Dance Floor :: Chris Tomlin

dating. One afternoon while we were picking out a Redbox, I knew it was time to tell Chad about that conversation I had with God. (There is never really a good time, is there?) So, in an awkward, yet relieving moment, I looked at Chad and started to explain, "I told God I'm not kissing until I'm married." Chad looked at me and said the most incredible thing, "God told me to do the same thing last week."

Physical boundaries in dating can be vague, to say the least. Everyone wants to know "how far is too far?" When my friend asked our youth pastor, he replied, "Whatever you can do in front of your dad will pass. If not, it's crossing a line." Sound radical? Maybe radical is good.

Chad recently talked with a friend who was losing the

battle to staying physically pure with his girlfriend. Chad asked what they typically do while hanging out. He explained how they watch movies alone until 1 a.m. *(Excuse me, did I hear that correctly? One in the morning?!?)* Chad had pinpointed the problem. If trouble is going to happen it will probably happen late at night! (Even Cinderella had a curfew with her prince!)

Love does not consist in gazing at each other, but in looking together in the same direction.
~Antoine de Saint-Exupery

When Chad and I brought home that Redbox, we created a plan *in advance* for purity. It started with agreeing on physical boundaries, early curfews and requesting accountability from others in our lives.

So how do you stay pure? When I'm riding down the highway, I reach for the dial to find my favorite radio station. I know the frequency, and once I've tuned in, the signal is loud and clear. It's just like this with God. If we're tuned in to hear Him speak, He will show us the path to purity.

REFLECTION & ACTION

1. Take a shot at memorizing this: "Don't copy the behavior and customs of this world, but let God transform you into a new person by changing the way you think. Then you will learn to know God's will for you, which is

good and pleasing and perfect" Romans 12:2 (NLT).

BOUND·A·RY
[boun-duh-ree]
something that indicates the farthest limit

2. Ask God what your physical boundaries in future relationships should be. Write down what He shares with you:

3. What kind of boundaries do you hope your future husband is making if he dates other girls?

ROMANS 14:13
GALATIANS 5:16-17

WEARING white

RACHEL COULD NOT BELIEVE what was happening to her. When the pregnancy test came up positive, the senior year she had always dreamed about came crashing down. Friends were talking and people she didn't even know were giving her looks.

Shame hit her like arrows darting through the halls.

Rachel's high school sweetheart stood by her, but life was altogether messy. Hand in hand they approached her parents with the news. Their reaction led to another flood of humiliation.

As the year closed, Rachel's boyfriend proposed. They hurried to plan a simple but beautiful wedding. Driving with her mom to find a wedding dress, her mom asked, "What color will your dress be?" Rachel contemplated it while the car hummed. "White." "Really?" her mom scoffed. The tone and rejection in her mom's voice resounded in Rachel's heart.

A few years ago, I glimpsed a picture of the kind of grace that Rachel's heart longed for. I was

your past mistakes don't define you or your future.

walking in my sacred place, which happens to be a path that lines the shores of southern England. I'm captivated by the waves crashing on the shore. They pull the salt water back and forth to reveal perfect, silken sand.

Speechless :: The Sonflowerz
Second Chance :: Rend Collective Experiment
Forgiven :: Sanctus Real

What the waves do for the shore is a picture of what the blood of Jesus does for us. It was His death on the cross that gives us a completely new beginning.

Not only did His sacrifice secure our eternity with Him, but every day, every minute, His blood washes us, leaving us blameless in God's eyes. Yes, blameless!

Romans 8 is my favorite chapter in the Bible. It affirms that we are no longer under the power of sin and shame: "With the arrival of Jesus, the Messiah . . . those who enter into Christ's being-here-for-us no longer have to live under a continuous, low-lying black cloud. A new power is in operation. The Spirit of life in Christ, like a strong wind, has magnificently cleared the air, freeing you from a fated lifetime of brutal tyranny at the hands of sin and death" (Romans 8:1–2, The Message).

Just as the waves wash the shore of any old footprints, so our past mistakes are erased when we believe in Jesus. He is the One who has removed our sins from us as far

i've heard it said

It's not as important how we start, but how we finish.
~Joyce Meyer

as the east is from the west (Psalm 103:12).

Any voices in our heads that condemn us can be silenced by this powerful truth. Your past mistakes don't define you or your future.

Sixteen years after that car ride with her mom, I was listening to Rachel tell her story. She'd become a mom with four kids and her high school sweetheart was still by her side. Despite the years that had passed, she still felt the sting of shame left from that drive to buy her dress.

Tears fell as she told the painful memory. Silence filled the room. Then, someone asked her, "Where was Jesus when you were riding in that car?" Rachel's tears subsided and a smile slowly surfaced. As a Christ-follower, she knew Jesus had been sitting right beside her, not accusing her, but defending her. He had always been there.

Maybe I should ask you the same question. When you went through your hardest moments, where do you see Jesus?

We've got nothing to lose but the shame! Jesus is on our side. He turns the page for a new chapter in our life. We are spotless, always wearing white because of Him.

REFLECTION & ACTION

1. Write a journal entry about any shame that clings to you. Ask God to forgive you and to take away the feelings of guilt and shame that you live with.

2. Open your fridge and pour a sip of grape juice into a glass, then grab one cracker to remember the death of Jesus. Read Matthew 26:26–28, the story of the first time this act of Communion took place. Finding a quiet place, ask God to remind you of the amazing sacrifice Jesus made so you could live free of shame. Because of Jesus's sacrifice for you, you have been made entirely acceptable to God (2 Corinthians 5:21).

3. Jesus is coming back for us and we are His bride—wearing white because He has made us blameless. Check out the scene in Revelation 7:9–12.

BLAME·LESS
[bleym-lis]
free from blame;
innocent

EPHESIANS 1:5–8
COLOSSIANS 1:13–14
PHILIPPIANS 3:13–15

my thoughts

WHEN MY DAD CAME DOWNSTAIRS to tell me I had a delivery at the door, I skipped every other stair to get there as fast as I could. A slender box addressed to me was on the piano. I bent the lid to reveal a red bouquet. Roses? From who? I searched for a note but only found a card that read "To Rebecca." Astonishment and intrigue brought me to a point of giddy excitement. I arranged the roses in water and called all my friends, hoping they could reveal the mystery.

But still nothing.

I spent the rest of the evening racking my brain. There was no boyfriend. No admirer that I knew of. I began to wonder if they came to the wrong address.

Have you ever received a gift like this? How did it make you feel?

Flowers on our doorstep are traditionally meant to say "I love you." But within a week, this gift began to wilt. And just as flowers fade, chocolates get devoured and teddy bears are stuffed in a closet. Suddenly the feelings those gifts bring dwindle away. You feel empty again.

Before you could prove anything, or do anything for Him, God made the statement "I love you."

What's the solution for our ever-forgetful hearts? One moment we are blissfully romanced and the next we are shrouded in longing. But there is one place where love is sustained, never flickering like a candle in the wind. It's the love God embodies. It's Him.

TODAY'S PLAYLIST

Revolutionary Love :: David Crowder Band
What Love Is This :: Kari Jobe
Relentless :: Hillsong United

Before you could prove anything, or do anything for Him, God made the statement "I love you." He has given us the gift of His love and scattered clues everywhere!

So what is so extraordinary about this love? Can it really top a dozen roses?

One morning in Medford, Oregon, we left early to catch a plane home. On the way out, our host, Cyndi, told us about a stop we could make on the way to the airport. It was a sight that people drive hours to see.

A tulip farm. Yep.

About three hours later we turned off the interstate. A small sign pointed the way down a dirt road. We turned in and pulled up to a man waiting in his booth, asking for five bucks to park.

By this time we were all eager to see what we tried to picture in our minds! Would it be worth the five bucks? Finally, walking to the top of a hill, there it was.

Rows of tulips for *miles*. Every color and variety you

could dream up! These were nothing like the store-bought kind. More than twice the size! I thought for a split second I had walked into another world, a scene described in fairy tales.

Joining the other visitors who had found this treasure off the beaten path, we marched up and down each row, crouching down for pictures. I breathed in the fragrance. My eyes had never seen so many colors in one place.

Our flight beckoned us and we made our way back to the parking lot. I thought back to the roses delivered to my door years ago. Next to these acres of beauty, a modest bouquet would pale in comparison! The kind gesture, though thoughtful, was still a borrowed bouquet. God, the creator of everything, owns the fields. He is the author of true beauty.

Do you know you are "be-loved"? Created to *be loved.* God goes public in Jeremiah 31:3: "I have loved you with an everlasting love; I have drawn you with unfailing kindness."

Staring back at the fields of color a final time, they seemed endless. No fence in sight. Then it dawned on me. That's how to describe God's love for us. It's limitless.

God's love isn't a theory. Like the tulips I could touch

and feel as they danced in the wind, it's a reality. He demonstrated this profound love in Jesus. When we know God, really know Him, we naturally run to Him. God is love, and love is a magnet!

To this day I don't know who sent the roses. I have my guesses, but the giver never showed. The love Jesus gives you and me never runs out. He is more reliable than a boyfriend or a best friend, or anyone else, for that matter.

REFLECTION & ACTION

1. Next time you run across a field of wildflowers, spend a minute to breathe in their fragrance. Remember God's love for you.

2. Read 1 Corinthians 13:4–8. Where you read the word "love," insert "Jesus." Have you ever read it this way before?

3. If you're like me, you need a kick start to get you opening the Word in the morning. Start with Ephesians 1, which sets the stage for understanding God's love for you. It's one of my favorites.

EVER·LAST·ING
[ev-er-las-ting]
never coming to an end, eternal

JOHN 17:26
PSALM 86:15
EPHESIANS 2:4

my thoughts

what about trueLOVE?

TO FIND THE MAN OF YOUR DREAMS, everyone says you've got to follow your heart. Movies portray love stories that are driven by emotions and serendipitous events where true love is the ultimate end. They walk into the sunset, and then the credits roll! Is this really an accurate picture of true love? Is it all about your emotions? Does dating come down to whether or not a guy makes you weak in the knees?

I recently attended an engagement party for my close friends Ben and Kristen. A homemade button with the bride-to-be's future initials adorned her blouse. Together they spilled the proposal story out to us, pausing between laughter and tears.

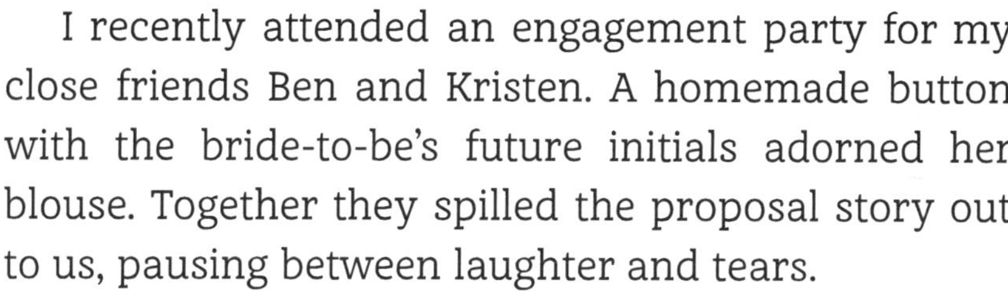

With both of their families at their side, it was a landmark moment for this couple. The bling on her finger wasn't a fashion statement, but a reminder of all the hard choices they had made to get them to their engagement day. Their relationship was based on more than a mushy feeling.

For years they prayed that God would be the leader in their relationship. That also meant waiting until their parents gave their blessing to the engagement

and future marriage. That took some time, but they were patient. Ben and Kristen walked out the words of Ephesians 6:2–3: "Honor your father and mother—which is the first commandment with a promise—so that it may go well with you and that you may enjoy long life on the earth."

TODAY'S PLAYLIST

Holding Nothing Back :: Ryan Stevenson
Get Back Up :: TobyMac
I Will Follow :: Chris Tomlin

My best friend Lauren called me from her apartment in Portland when she got engaged. We giggled like we were five again. His proposal was every girl's dream! On the beach. *At sunset.* But the larger story of these two falling in love also involved her spiritual mentors' counsel at every stage. Lauren's parents aren't people of faith; so walking out Ephesians 6:2–3 meant she and Matt sought out adults they trusted as spiritual guides. They came to them with questions on a regular basis and prayed together.

The bling on her finger wasn't a fashion statement, but a reminder of all the hard choices they had made.

When the wedding invitation came in the mail, I booked my flight to be there. I sat sipping punch at their reception while Lauren's mentor gave a toast, gushing with excitement and stories. My friend sparkled with joy.

Is it all about true love? Well, it's bigger than that. Surrounding yourself with wise counselors is essential to getting off to a winning start in your future marriage. Just ask Lauren or Kristen!

How do you get from where you are now to the crescendo of the perfect wedding? It's no small thing to decide to trust God, making Him the director of your love life, prayerfully committing with the psalmist, "Hour by hour I place my days in your hands" (Psalm 31:15, The Message).

What does it look like for God to lead your dating relationship? **BE SPECIFIC**

If you are in a relationship right now and you have accountability through your youth pastor, parents, or a spiritual mentor, you're already on a roll. Seeking God individually on a regular basis will keep you on track. I can already visualize the bridesmaids lined up in purple dresses and the flower girl's rose petals floating through the air at Ben and Kristen's wedding. They will have the greatest joy because they chose to entrust their lives to an all-knowing God, who faithfully directs our steps—even the steps we take in relationships.

REFLECTION & ACTION

1. What's your relationship status?

2. Make a list of the people in your life who give you counsel in your relationships:

3. What's your next move to involve God, and even your parents, in your love life decisions?

PROVERBS 2:1-10
1 TIMOTHY 6:6

I WAS ON A WALK WITH MY MOM down a well-worn jogging path by the neighborhood creek. Not far off, a family was coming toward us from the other direction. Three kids were barreling down upon us on bikes. We scooted over to give them more room.

As the two older brothers led the way, we got a good look at a young girl with cherry red cheeks doing everything in her power to keep up with them. Her long curly locks were thrown back by the wind, and the set of training wheels keeping her upright bounced over the gravel.

She whirled past us and I glanced back. *How cute,* I thought. Suddenly she flung her head back and shouted out in the greatest triumph, "I'm living the DREAM life!"

My mom and I giggled . . . and giggled some more. Long after the family was out of sight, we were still talking about this girl with red cheeks.

The way we're wired, worries and dreams about the future can easily swallow up our present joys.

What is the dream life anyway? Her words seemed to stick with me, and the timing was perfect.

I had been so tangled up with worry that the here-and-now was beginning to feel like grunt work. Each day, all I could think of was the huge pile of stuff I had to do. But the dream life isn't about those things. In fact, I had lost sight of the dreams that mattered to me.

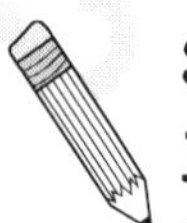

So, what's your idea of a dream life?

JOT IT DOWN

It's as if Jesus is speaking right to me when He says, "Give your entire attention to what God is doing right now, and

TODAY'S PLAYLIST

This Is Your Life :: Switchfoot
Dreamer :: Bethany Dillon
God of Our Salvation :: Phil Wickham

don't get worked up about what may or may not happen tomorrow. God will help you deal with whatever hard things come up when the time comes" (Matthew 6:34, The Message).

In other words, don't worry about tomorrow. But worry was all my mind had been stuck on until this tricycle-riding wake-up call appeared.

What about you? There are decisions to make. Who will you invite to your next party, or will you introduce yourself to that boy in your class? Or in a few years the questions will be about college and finding a job

The future belongs to those who believe in the beauty of their dreams.
~ Eleanor Roosevelt

or a place to live. At some point, you might be making a choice about who to marry. Does worry fill these spaces in your life?

Now I know why Jesus told us not to worry about our future. The way we're wired, worries and dreams about the future can easily swallow up our present joys.

What if I told you that you are living your dream life *now*? When Jesus taught His followers to be like little children, I think He wanted us to trust the Father completely. Can you see yourself, like that five-year-old, yelling out, "I'm living the dream life!"? (Try it now! 1...2...3... Go!)

Now that you've yelled out loud and spooked the dog, here's the most essential element to it all: "Seek first his kingdom and his righteousness, and all these things will be given to you as well" (Matthew 6:33).

As I make my life about God's concerns and not my own, He will take care of the rest.

Not long after I saw that wild little bike girl, I decided to make a resolution to yell out "I'm living the dream life!" anywhere and everywhere: elevators, football fields, inside the car wash. . . I want to be like that joy-riding girl, celebrating what my Father in Heaven has done for me each day.

JOY
[joi]
a deep feeling or condition of happiness or contentment

REFLECTION & ACTION

1. Have your goals for the future got you spinning into discontentment in the present? List your worries.

2. Read Jeremiah 29:11. How does this promise keep you from worry?

PSALM 55:22
ROMANS 8:28

my thoughts

GLOW

[glo]

1. to give out steady light without flame

2. a steady radiance of light or heat

THERE ARE DAYS WHEN I'm the sister you don't want to be around. I call them "drama queen days." I'm in one of my girl moods, and Cheetos are liable to be thrown across the room! I'm likely to be found alone somewhere playing my guitar.

It can hit me on a long tour, as claustrophobia overtakes me in the van. Things can get unpleasant—to put it lightly. Yes, we're real people (ask Becca!).

When I was younger, these intense emotions came out around friends. Too bad for them! Call me a drama queen or just "sensitive." Either way, I'm not afraid to express how I feel.

Now, this *can* be a good thing, because I will be the last person to bottle things up and then explode! But, this drama was not the best God intended for me. You know that thing called "self control" we read about in Galatians 5:23? That is what I needed to acquire.

God's Spirit—you know, the One living inside of you—is there to bring peace into every square inch of our lives. Drama doesn't have to define us!

Stand your ground in love and patience.

Isaiah, a truth-telling prophet from the Bible, explains what God's Spirit is meant to do in us when we entrust ourselves to Him. "You will guard him and keep him in perfect and constant peace whose mind is stayed on You, because he commits himself to You, leans on You, and hopes confidently in You" (Isaiah 26:3, Amplified Bible).

TODAY'S PLAYLIST

Something Holy :: Stellar Kart
Restless :: Audrey Assad
Remedy :: Rachael Lampa

What do you do when your friend is crowned the drama queen? Let me tell you (from the perspective of one) to hang in there, girl; this friend of yours requires a lot of patience. But you are in luck, because patience is something God wants stored up in us. On the other hand, being easily offended by her is like a time bomb waiting to take you out.

Stand your ground in love and patience. In a matter of time, everything that was a huge deal to her will dissipate and emotions will settle.

What drama have you encountered within your close relationships?

JOT IT DOWN

A drama queen is a person who often has exaggerated or overly emotional reactions to events or situations.

Drama can be addicting to the person creating it. Your biggest challenge is not to let yourself be pulled into it.

Jesus teaches those who want to follow Him, "Blessed are the peacemakers, for they will be called children of God" (Matthew 5:9). As you start to notice a situation that has more drama than necessary, look to God. He will answer your prayer for wisdom every time. Through Scripture and people you trust, and even through creative God-ideas, He will show you how to be a peacemaker.

There may be occasions where the friend drama is just too intense. When it starts to drag you down, it is okay to step back from a drama queen. But keep praying for her. God has a reason for bringing her into your life.

REFLECTION & ACTION

1. Is there a drama queen in your life that drives you crazy? Ask God how you can show His love to this person.

2. Are *you* the drama queen? (Come on. Be honest!) Taking steps toward real peace and self-control starts with asking God to help you.

3. Take a minute to pray for the relationships in your life that are strained by drama.

PEACE·MAK·ER
[pees-mey-ker]
someone who tries to make peace, especially by reconciling parties who disagree

ROMANS 8:6
JOHN 14:1

"IT'S THE BIG THING RIGHT NOW!" A group of my friends were clustered around a copy of *Seventeen* magazine, pouring over a long list of rules for becoming popular. I knew many of them were already working through rule number five. Then the subject turned to which scary movie to rent and how to get a date with the hottest boy in class. Despite their shallow and skewed perspective, it was way too easy to join in. After all, friends stick together, right?

But, we didn't see eye to eye and before long I had to turn a corner. Truthfully, I felt lonely in my choices to stand apart from the buzz-hopping crowd. Following God meant gutsy decisions to go the opposite way. And that *wasn't* easy.

Whether you realize it or not, you are sending a bold message to others by your choices. My friends learned I wouldn't buckle under their so-called peer pressure. They started leaving me out, not inviting me to that movie, that joyride, that sleepover. Perhaps they thought I was lame. Or they knew I would speak out, and they didn't want a guilt trip.

There are defining moments in our lives, and this was one for me. I heard these words, "Enter through the narrow gate. For wide is the gate and broad is the road that leads to destruction, and many enter through it. But small is the gate and narrow the road that leads to life, and only a few find it" (Matthew 7:13–14).

TODAY'S PLAYLIST

The Opposite Way :: Leeland
All Over The World :: The Sonflowerz
Overcomer :: Mandisa

The question is raised for us today. Are we up for the fight that comes with walking what Jesus calls "the narrow road"?

It's probably pretty simple to picture the wide road, because those are the choices that a lot of others at school are making—choices like sleeping around and drinking. It takes more guts, though, to walk the narrow road.

What kind of peer pressure have you dealt with?

DESCRIBE IT HERE

A lot of girls feel conflicted over decisions like:

- How they should dress
- How much they should weigh
- Lying to their parents
- Wanting the trendy stuff their friends have

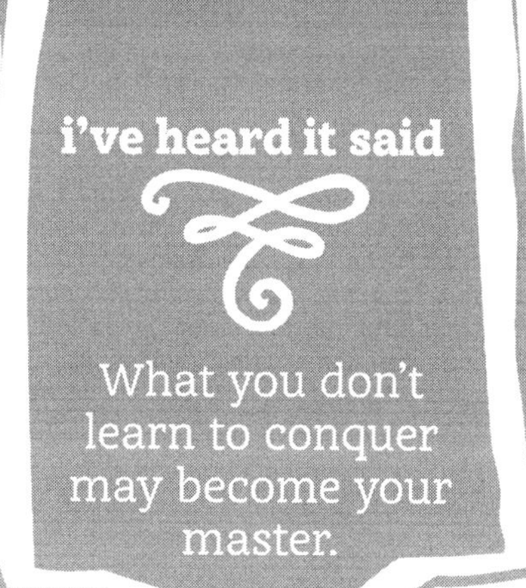

- Hanging out with people they're not comfortable with

I can go down this list and think of a time (or several) where I battled with a choice. Lie to my parents, or tell them the truth. Wear what I want, or think about the message I'm sending. And the list could go on.

I wouldn't have lasted long on the narrow road if it weren't for God's Spirit. He's the One you can't see with your eyes, the One who lives inside you and is your source of strength to stand up for what you know is right. Have you needed Him lately? I have.

You were made for so much more than following the whims of those around you.

A friend of mine, author Vicki Courtney, says, "Self-control, apart from the power of Christ, is futile." This means that my will power will eventually fail! It's only God's help in my life that enables me to stand up to every kind of peer pressure, even if I feel urged to do it.

And, let me tell you, you were made for so much more than following the whims of those around you. God has things in store for you that will blow your mind—but there's a catch: you gotta choose the narrow road to find them.

The moment you are faced with a choice isn't the time to figure out how good decisions come about. You need to plan ahead, girl! So before you get there, here's a strategy of how to truly "fight like a girl" . . . and WIN:

Stop. Think. Pray. Three little words that pack a punch.

STOP—don't jump into situations. Take a minute to make a right-on decision.

THINK—consider the implications and what the Bible lays out for you. (Read it regularly so verses come to mind!)

PRAY—this is the key to discovering good choices! Prayer is essentially asking God to guide you. Then trust Him to show you what to do. He *will* give you a way out.

In 2 Peter 1:6, Peter, an extraordinary leader in the early church, sums up the formula for self-control: Knowing God leads to self-control. Self-control leads to patient endurance, and patient endurance leads to godliness. Essentially, self-control is a byproduct of knowing God—and it's a result of the Spirit living inside you! (Galatians 5:22–23)

So, who is guiding your decisions? Do your more outgoing friends make your choices for you? Girls with a take-charge attitude tend to influence their friends, good or bad. If you're happy taking a back seat and letting others lead the way, you could be giving into peer pressure without knowing it.

But you also have the opportunity to lead. Show your friends—show everyone—what it looks like to walk the narrow road.

EN·DUR·ANCE
[en-door-uhns]
the ability or strength to continue or last, especially despite fatigue

REFLECTION & ACTION

1. People who follow Jesus, trying to live like Him, are described as "strangers on earth" in Hebrews 11:13. Have you embraced this identity, or are you still trying to be like the world around you?

2. Today, when faced with a challenging choice, put "**STOP**, **THINK**, and **PRAY**" into practice.

PROVERS 3:13-14
JAMES 3:17

3. Read Matthew 26:41 and pray for God's strength and wisdom when you are tempted.

sisters

I ONCE HAD A MONUMENTAL conversation with a friend that I'll never forget. She and her sisters had started a band at the same time we did.

We were on the deck of a beautiful home overlooking the grand mountain range surrounding Vail, Colorado. Breathtaking.

We talked about the way that intertwining sisterhood with band life can open a bit of jealousy. Comparisons and careless remarks between sisters can create division of the worst kind. My friend confided in me that God had been asking her to shut the door on envy.

Through her confession, God had a message for my heart, too. My friend told me to embrace my role in the band and never become jealous of my sister's role or gifts. Everything inside me knew she was right. It was pivotal.

I was the star soccer player and the outgoing member of my family. But starting a band with my sister meant being more of a team player. I couldn't fight for center stage. That weekend I said a simple prayer, expressing my heart to God. "I'm

> *Comparisons and careless remarks between sisters can create a division of the worst kind.*

giving this to You," I said. "I need your grace and strength to be satisfied in the role You have given me. I choose to be humble, to serve, to work as a team, and to do it ultimately for Your glory, not mine."

Jealousy creeps in subtly, beginning with thoughts like, "I wish I had what she has," or, "She doesn't deserve that as much as I do." But at its core, jealousy is accusing God of not providing what we need. We look at what others have and feel dissatisfied with our portion. It's weighing our "have-nots" with their "haves."

TODAY'S PLAYLIST

Let Us Love :: Needtobreathe
You Deserve :: Hillsong United
Learn to Love :: Leeland

Any situation can breed discontent if we're not aware of what's going on within the corridors of our heart. Girls, "Let us not become conceited, provoking and envying each other" (Galatians 5:26).

What is one way you can break away from jealousy toward your friends or siblings?

I'm a decorating fanatic, always hanging posters on my wall. One has written on it the words of 1 Corinthians 13—the chapter of the Bible most famous for describing perfect love: "Love is patient, love is kind. It does not envy, it does not boast, it is not proud. . ." If we are envious of our friends, we are far from loving them.

Have you let jealous thoughts bully you around? It's time to stand up to that thinking and make a switch. Envy develops into judgment, and pretty soon you can resent your friends for who they are.

Love is the reset button. We are all just seconds away from pushing that button to start fresh! Before envy enters and takes root, ask God to give you love for your friends or siblings. Ask Him to show you that He's met all your needs. It's not found in being like someone else or having what they have.

That whole weekend in Vail was thrilling, but I will always remember the conversation on the deck. My friend's story of overcoming jealousy between sisters resonated with me. I decided to let go, too, and see sisterhood in a totally different light.

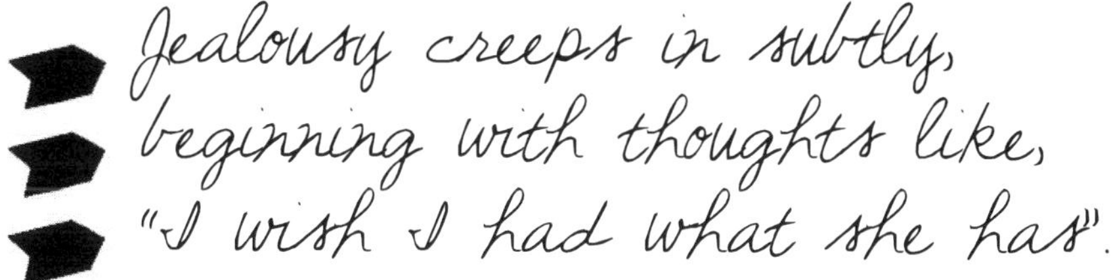

REFLECTION & ACTION

1. Write down **two** reasons you don't want to be envious of others.

1

2

2. Read 1 Peter 4:8. Spend time praying for any person you feel envious towards. Ask God to give you His love for them.

1 PETER 1:22
JOHN 13:34

70x7

WHY IS FORGIVING someone so hard? It feels like climbing uphill with the wind and rain charging against me. Every step is a challenge, a choice. But if forgiveness is like a summit, it is more liberating than anything to reach the top.

Becca and I were talking to students at a boarding school in England when the topic of forgiveness came up. I asked the British girl sitting beside me how she saw it. To her, forgiveness would only be given if someone *deserved* it.

On the days when I open my inbox to read a nasty email, or when a crazy driver almost runs me off the road, forgiveness is a challenge. For a split second I wished that the British girl was right, and I only had to forgive occasionally. Holding a grudge is easier, right?

Have you ever met a truly bitter person? Negativity and discouragement eat up everything in their path. It's like a weight they swing around a room causing destruction everywhere.

Choosing not to forgive causes bitterness to fester. And festering is not a pretty thing. Medical research has even shown that bitterness can cause

> *If forgiveness is like a summit, it is more liberating than anything to reach the top.*

physical sickness, depression, anxiety, and chronic pain![1]

With all that said, have you ever held onto a grudge? What effect did it have on your friendship with the person you resented?

In high school, my friend found out the effects of bitterness in a very real way. She hated her dad for leaving

The War Inside :: Switchfoot
There Is A Redeemer :: The Sonflowerz
Forgiven :: Sanctus Real

her mom and having an affair. I sat with her for hours talking through it and still she wouldn't let go of her anger against him. As stomach ulcers and ruined relationships plagued her, she eventually gave up and began to forgive. Holding the grudge hurt more than the initial reason for her anger. It separated her from her family and left her feeling miserable.

As I watched my friend go through this, God showed me that I wasn't the one to rescue her from it all, He was. I stepped back, prayed for her, and in time I saw healing begin in her heart. Our friendship was reestablished when we had both worked through forgiveness.

> Forgiveness is to set a prisoner free, and to *realize* the prisoner was *you*.
> **~ Corrie Ten Boom**

My friend, a daughter once distanced by hate, went to her dad for forgiveness as well. Like a flower about to bloom, the outcome was peace, love, and the sweetest freedom. Their relationship is strong today.

Forgiving someone who has harmed us is a long journey. But Jesus tells us to keep forgiving, even if it's seventy-times-seven times! (That's 490 times, if you're doing the math.)

Still want a better reason to bother forgiving your greatest enemy? Here it is in Colossians 3:13: "Bear with each other and forgive one another if any of you has a grievance [complaint] against someone. Forgive as the Lord forgave you."

Negativity and discouragement eat up everything in their path. It's like a weight they swing around a room.

If for no other reason, forgive because Jesus walked a long, painful road to forgive *your* sin—including the bitterness that comes with unforgiveness! He's not counting your record of wrongs, so why should we count the records of others?

Do you or I deserve forgiveness? Not one bit. But Jesus did it anyway. He wiped the slate clean for us, and never remembers our sin. I'm so amazed at this! And He raises the bar by saying this is what we are to do for others.

We see Jesus on the cross in Luke 23:34, just before His last breath, forgiving those who crucified Him. This depth of forgiveness is something that astounds me. Girls, it takes nothing less than God's power working in us to achieve it. The person who never gives up forgiving will most definitely reach the summit, and the climb will be worth every step.

REFLECTION & ACTION

1. Read Matthew 18:21–33

2. List the names of people you are in process of forgiving, and take a minute to pray about it.

[1] http://www.mayoclinic.com/health/forgiveness/MH00131

3. Read Philippians 1:6. What does this say to you about the "work of forgiveness" that we invite God to do in us?

RE·SENT·MENT
[ri-zent-muhnt]
anger, bitterness, ill will

PSALM 103:3
MATTHEW 6:12

my thoughts

day 25

DEFEATING depression

THE MESSAGE POPPED UP from a teen in Michigan: "I'm pretty depressed." That same day I got a phone call from my friend who was grieving her dad's death: "I don't know what to do; I'm so depressed."

Depression hits us for different reasons and stays for undetermined amounts of time. Talk about unexpected and unwelcomed! Webster's dictionary defines depression as "a condition of general emotional dejection and withdrawal." As girls, even the hormones in our bodies have the potential to make us feel low on certain days of the month.

So, when was the last time you were depressed and why? **DESCRIBE IT HERE**

As I watch people around me suffer in this way, I'm convinced this is a serious issue. There are different causes for depression—sometimes it's hormonal or a chemical imbalance, sometimes it's circumstantial, and other times it's a spiritual battle.

I was feeling the "D-word" last week. It evolved out of a number of outrageous situations that were beyond my control. I let out a frustrated prayer in the shower. (Admit it, you do it too.) "Ahhh! I'm so upset, God. Why can't things in life be easier?"

Honestly, I don't always hear from God every time I pray, but in that moment a fresh understanding of

Light It Up :: For King & Country
In You Alone :: The Sonflowerz
Strangely Dim :: Francesca Battistelli

my situation came to me. Right in the middle of my complaining, He said, "If you would just look to My face . . . " Could seeing His face really wash every thought of depression away?

Helen Lemmel penned the words of this song:

Turn your eyes upon Jesus.
Look full in His wonderful face,
and the things of this world will grow
strangely dim,
in the light of His glory and grace.

Maybe our answer is hidden there!

What does it really mean to see the face of Jesus? It means experiencing Him in such a personal way that it wipes the table clean of every aching, depressing thought. And this heart-glimpse of God is the reminder that we are not alone—Jesus is with us through the hard stuff.

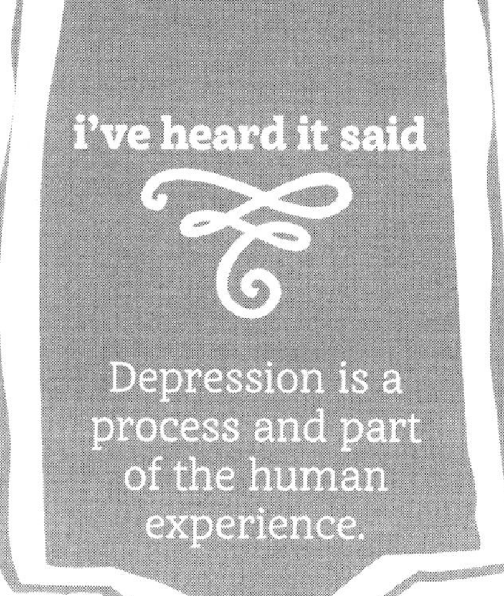

The writer of Psalm 42 has hit rock bottom in his life and opens in desperation, "My soul thirsts for God, for the living God. When can I go and meet with God? My tears have been my food day and night, while people say to me all day long, 'Where is your God?' Why, my soul, are you downcast? Why so disturbed within me? Put your hope in God, for I will yet praise Him, my Savior and my God."

The writer turns his heart towards hope and praise at the conclusion. Worshiping God brings gratefulness out of our hearts. Being thankful can combat depression in our lives, even when it's the last thing we feel like doing. And though we can't actually see God, He revolutionizes our hearts every time we shove the world away just to be with Him.

Right in the middle of my complaining, He said, "If you would just look to My face . . ."

Ten minutes spent focusing my mind and heart on God redirects my entire day, and plants seeds inside me for a future that's upbeat and cheerful. (Like a good song!)

Why do we leave God out of our emotional misery when He desperately wants to be invited in?

REFLECTION & ACTION

1. List some things you are thankful for:

2. What are some ways you can meet with God during a period of depression? Set up a plan for the next time you feel low.

THANK·FUL
[thangk-fuhl]
expressing gratitude, appreciation

3. I imagine Jesus' followers could have been depressed after witnessing the death of their leader and best friend. They mourned for three days, but then, Jesus rose from the dead. Their hearts were lifted *when they saw His face*. Read Luke 24:30–35.

4. Talk to a trusted adult or a counselor if you can't shake your depression or have thoughts of suicide. Your fight against depression could be a spiritual one. Check out what Ephesians 6:11-17 has to say.

PSALM 61:1-4
PHILIPPIANS 4:6-7

my thoughts

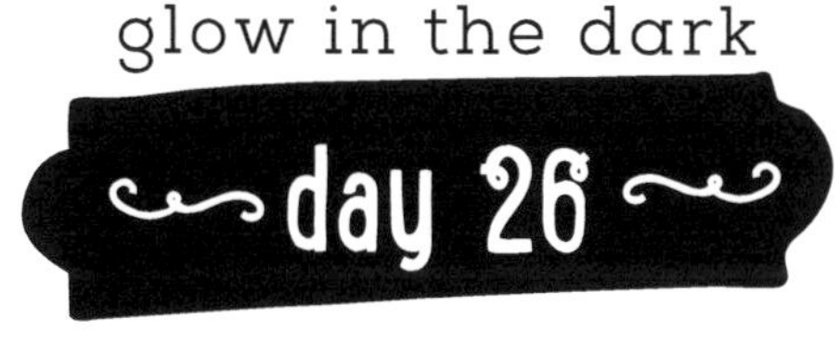

BATTLEGROUNDS

I CAN PICTURE RECESS at my elementary school like it was yesterday. Nick, abnormally taller than everyone else in our class, spent his free time throwing verbal punches my way. He called my nine-year-old self "skinny bones." Translation? Weak. Pathetic. *Just* a girl.

Never was I more surprised when I saw him one weekend at a Christian concert. "Hypocrite!" I said under my breath. His words the next day on the playground stung even more. I *so* wanted to fight back and make him feel ashamed about how he treated me.

Each morning my mom drove Elissa and me down the interstate to school, crossing jam-packed lanes of traffic. As she drove our boxy grey minivan, she reminded us of the words in Ephesians 6, the inventory of the armor of God, and together we recited each line. Imagine hearing this in a British accent (since Mom is from London) as you take inventory yourself: "A final word: be strong in the Lord and in his mighty power. Put on all of God's armor so that you will be able to stand firm against all strategies of the devil. For we are not fighting

{God's word is my sword}

against flesh-and-blood enemies, but against evil rulers and authorities of the unseen world" (Ephesians 6:10–12, NLT). No doubt, those verses built up my courage. I walked into school with an invisible shield over my heart.

The battle I encountered had never been with Nick or a crew of catty girls. It was against the enemy of my soul, trying to tear me down.

Overcome :: Jeremy Camp
The Proof Of Your Love :: For King & Country
Face The Son :: The Sonflowerz

Identifying my real enemy helped me find a way to be kind at school—even, maybe (possibly!), to love my classmates as God does.

The inventory continues in verses 14–15, "Stand your ground, putting on the belt of truth and the body armor of God's righteousness. For shoes, put on the peace that comes from the Good News so that you will be fully prepared. In addition to all of these, hold up the shield of faith to stop the fiery arrows of the devil. Put on salvation as your helmet, and take the sword of the Spirit, which is the word of God."

Have you considered the unseen spiritual battles that are being fought all around you each day? What are you doing to win those battles? Describe what you are doing on the following page.

WHAT'S YOUR BATTLEPLAN?

> A girl is like
> a tea bag—
> you can't tell how
> strong she is
> until you put her
> in hot water.
> **~Eleanor Roosevelt**

Your fight may look different from the one I faced at school. Maybe you are bombarded by dark thoughts in your own mind. Or maybe your siblings are pointing their fingers your way. What will you do in defense?

When we acknowledge that these are real spiritual battles, and that our enemy, the devil, is behind these thoughts, we can resist them by the authority that Jesus gives us. "Submit yourselves, then, to God. Resist the devil and he will flee from you" (James 4:7).

And why not invite others into combat with you? Your trusted friends, who are on this same path following Jesus, are your reminders that you're not alone in this fight. If you've been trying to overcome serious struggles on

Your fight may look different from the one I encountered at school.

your own, maybe it's time to ask your youth pastor, your parents, or a close friend to pray with you. I guarantee, this is one of the reasons God has put them in your life!

My battles no longer deal with name-calling, and I haven't seen Nick in years (which I'm slightly relieved about), but I still face opposition. When I do, I remember the words in Ephesians 6. I can still picture my mom gripping the wheel of our minivan, "Now girls, let's say it together . . ." That was years ago, but today I am prepared for any challenge because God's Word *is* my sword. My faith in Him, and His ability to overcome anything, is my shield. His Truth is secured tight around me like a belt. The helmet of salvation protects my mind, and my heart is guarded by His righteousness!

That's a full suitcase.

REFLECTION & ACTION

1. Challenge! Take a stab at memorizing Ephesians 6:10–17.

AR·MOR
[ahr-mer]
a covering worn as a defense against weapons

2. What is the biggest difficulty you face in your personal life? How can you stand strong according to Ephesians 6?

3. Think of **two** friends that struggle with personal battles, and spend a minute praying for them.

1

2

my thoughts

LIME·LIGHT

[lahym-lahyt]

1. intense white light obtained by heating a cylinder of lime, formally used in theatres

2. the focus of public attention

in the limelight

THERE'S A PHENOMENON HAPPENING in my city. Instead of a usual workout routine, people attempt to scale “the Incline”: a long, very steep old cable-car path that leads virtually *straight up* a Colorado mountainside.

It’s a rite of passage for athletes at the U.S. Olympic Training Center just down the road. Beginning at about 6,500 feet in elevation, the Incline takes you to 8,500 feet in less than a mile. Rows of unevenly spaced railroad ties make it a staircase up a mountain. It’s the equivalent of racing up the stairs of the Empire State Building—twice!

I feel tired just thinking about it.

Striving on our own, without God, is like taking on the Incline with a broken leg. Some days I feel like I’m trekking like this as I work feverishly to finish projects and find success in a world where the odds are against me.

Today I finally asked God, “Where do I go from here? I feel out of breath, like I can’t move forward or bear to look at the mountain ahead of me.”

Weakness rallies our dependence on God.

Do you ever feel like this?

Isaiah was a prophet from the Old Testament called by God to speak to the people of Israel. It was an overwhelming task, but God's hand constantly supported him. Aware of his own weakness, he wrote, "Those who wait upon God get fresh strength. They spread their wings and soar like eagles, they run and don't get tired, they walk and don›t lag behind" (Isaiah 40:31, The Message).

TODAY'S PLAYLIST

How Great You Are :: The Sonflowerz
Signature of Divine :: Needtobreathe
Ever Lifting :: Christy Nockels

Weakness rallies our dependence on God.

Has there been a time in your life when you have felt weak in your own ability?

I see my own weakness when I'm impatient with people or when I can't make good on the promise I made to a friend. I want to reach every goal I make for myself in ten seconds flat. It's just who I am! When I feel my frailty, it is an opportunity to stop and pray.

And if I'm honest, my prayers begin with frustration, wondering why I can't do everything with superhero strength. The truth is, I need Jesus. Desperately. He's better than anyone else at meeting needs. I'd much rather admit my weakness than climb a mountain without Him.

How does God's strength refresh us when we feel weak?

> **i've heard it said**
>
> It's the sides of the mountains that sustain life, not the top.

Does it happen like a lightning bolt—a zap of power—or more like a constant flowing river that we can drink from? Could it be that we don't need a one-time electric shock, but instead a daily intake of His presence?

Imagine God's strength as a pure, glistening stream, much like the ones I see on my drives into the Colorado mountains. This river of God is not going to run dry when drought hits. When I reach toward this stream—His word that never fails me, His voice that calms me—I am weak, but at the same time, strong. I confess to God that I don't have it in me, then He points to His Spirit in me and says, "Actually, yes it is in you. I am in You!"

Halfway up this daunting emotional Incline, I take a break to rest. My powerlessness is replaced by peace as I drink from this stream. God is strong in me in the midst of my frailty.

REFLECTION & ACTION

1. Read 1 Corinthians 1:25. Write about a time in your life when God became your strength.

2. Plan a hike with your family or a friend. As you climb uphill, think about the strength God offers you in life's ups and downs.

RE·FRESH·ING
[ri-fresh-ing]
serving to restore energy and vitality

2 CORINTHIANS 12:9
PSALM 59:17

in the limelight

first RESPONSE

DAD AND MOM WERE NEWLY MARRIED, living in a small town in Texas. Every night Dad drove home from his job in the city. One night Mom got a call that Dad had been in an accident, and she immediately knew that it was life-threatening.

A college student had been drinking with her friends and, thinking she could make it home, she took off down the pitch-black highway going the *wrong* direction. In his small Honda, Dad didn't see her speeding toward him until the moment the pickup truck in front of him swerved off the road.

The first responder in the middle of this dark night was a man who ran out of his nearby home at the sound of the huge crash. Because he called 911 immediately, he most likely saved my dad's life.

The drunk driver died instantly and Dad came very close, losing about eighty percent of his blood, breaking his jaw, femur, and left arm, and crushing his ankle. It took several top surgeons nine hours to piece his arm and jaw back together.

I was born a couple years later and I have never known Dad to be able to walk without a limp, let

There are a lot of responses we can have when we are at a colossal breaking point...

alone run. He has always had pain and some days it's worse than others. Still, in all my life, I have never heard Dad lash out in anger towards God about the accident or about his pain.

All This Time :: Britt Nicole
You Never Let Go :: Jeremy Camp
Forever Reign :: One Sonic Society

There are a lot of responses we can have when we are at a colossal breaking point. In the times you've encountered tragedy, what has been your first response towards God?

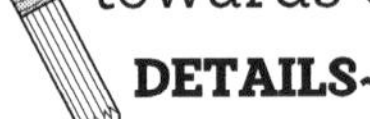

God understands frustrated and angry prayers. He walks with us through the grief. But, God isn't the author of pain or evil. A writer from the book of Psalms says, "God is our refuge and strength, an ever-present help in trouble. Therefore, we will not fear, though the earth give way and the mountains fall into the heart of the sea, though its waters roar and foam and the mountains quake with their surging" (Psalm 46:1-3). What circumstance represents "the earth giving way" in your life?

When the paramedics came to rescue my dad, they

God whispers to us in our pleasures, speaks to us in our conscience, but shouts in our pains: It is His megaphone to rouse a deaf world.
~C.S. Lewis

said it was a wonder he didn't injure his head or vital organs. My grandma recalls sensing a need to pray for her son that day—and God was listening.. No doubt angels were near! The doctors said it was a miracle dad survived.

Though some question God's love during tragedy, Dad became an unshakable man of faith because of his car accident. Certainly he wrestled with questions while he spent weeks in a hospital bed, but through it all he was convinced: God is real and He loves us no matter what. Dad always said that, this side of heaven, we may never fully understand why bad things happen. But, in His love, God gave us free will to *choose* to love Him in return. Otherwise, we'd be robots to God and He didn't want forced love, since true love is always voluntary. Free will is a gift, but it has ripple effects everywhere—some are terrible—when we, or others, make bad decisions, like the drunk driver that hit Dad.

God understands frustrated and angry prayers.

The Bible states emphatically that God is love. And in the next beat it says, "This is how God showed his love among us: he sent his one and only Son into the world that we might live through Him" (1 John 4:9). If we try to resolve whether or not God loves us by a car accident, or any painful circumstance, we are looking in the wrong place.

God made the most extravagant sacrifice by offering His life on the cross to show you that, forever and ever, He loves you. *Look at the cross.* Nothing is stronger than that sacrifice and the love God has for you.

REFLECTION & ACTION

1. Was there a time you blamed God for a bad situation in your life? Record it here:

2. What does Jesus dying on the cross mean to you?

REF·UGE
[ref-yooj]
a place or a person,
offering protection
of a safe shelter
from something

3. Read Romans 8:31-37 and write out your prayer to God in response to this passage.

my thoughts

in the limelight

courageous beauty

COURAGEOUS. It's a word that stirs up images of epic battle scenes like *Lord of the Rings*. Sacrifice. Perseverance. Total guy stuff. In each battle scene, the warrior fights through the fear that would try to defeat him.

Before you think that this kind of courage is reserved for guys, get to know a couple friends of mine. Meet Jaime, who left home to be a teacher in Southeast Asia, showing God's love to Buddhist families. Callie, who rides horses bareback, can be found in our state capitol building with a passion to change politics (after feeding her horses!).

Jaime and Callie will say that it wasn't easy to take courageous steps. For Jaime, living in a foreign land brought the fear of not fitting in and being alone. Callie devoted hours to studying and applying for internships.

Marching into the unknown and staring their fears in the face required trust in God–who is greater than anything we encounter!

Think about the most courageous thing you've ever done. Highlight some of the details in the space provided on the following page:

To live life in the way God intended, we can't remain frozen in fear.

Fear tells us to settle for what's easy. We've all faced it. But what we choose to do with our fears will determine our future. To live life in the way God intended, we can't remain frozen in fear.

TODAY'S PLAYLIST

By Faith :: The Sonflowerz
Set the World on Fire :: Britt Nicole
Called Me Higher :: All Sons & Daughters

Moses was a man with an extraordinary story. As a helpless baby, the house of the Egyptian Pharaoh adopted him. Later in life, he fled Egypt after murdering a man and spent years as a shepherd in the desert. During this time God came to Moses in a supernatural way, asking him to do something courageous.

Moses was enraptured by the burning bush that God spoke to him from, but it didn't erase the fears churning inside. Exodus chapter 4 recounts Moses telling God, "Send someone else," complaining that he wasn't good with words and always felt tongue-tied. Riddled with fear, he didn't want to go to Egypt to complete the assignment God was giving him!

Can you relate to Moses? Um, my hand is raised! Truth is,

when I'm on stage, fear shouts in my mind: *You're unqualified! You'll sound ridiculous!* But the craziest part is that I can sense God speaking over all the noise, calming my fears every time I step out.

i've heard it said

Feed your fears and your faith will starve. Feed your faith, and your fears will.
~ Max Lucado

Faith in God makes us courageous as we hang onto these words: "Since God assured us, 'I'll never let you down, never walk off and leave you,' we can boldly quote, 'God is there, ready to help; I'm fearless no matter what. Who or what can get to me?' " (Hebrews 13:6, The Message).

Faith is the exact opposite of fear. We will all be confronted with something that we feel unprepared for. God wants us to take on the challenge so our faith in Him can rise to the occasion.

Jaime and Callie are two inspirations of how to live courageously. Girls, it's time to be history makers! What's your next bold move?

REFLECTION & ACTION

1. Is there a particular fear that keeps you from saying "*yes*" to what God has called you to do?

2. Define **FAITH** in your own words:

3. Read Hebrews 11. What stands out to you the most?

in the limelight

by becca

I KNOW A GUY who just drools over his car. His Nissan Altima Coupe, to be specific. Even in the extreme winter, it stays polished to show off the metallic slate. I might even go so far as to say he worships his car.

Why? Everyone worships something, whether we know it or not. Not everyone's into Nissans. Instead, it could be the new iPhone, a boy band, the latest TV show, or money.

For us girls, the likely culprit might be that perfect appearance we spend hours achieving in front of the mirror or the popularity we sacrifice everything to have. We become worshipers of anything that consumes our time and thoughts.

We become worshipers of anything that consumes our time and thoughts.

I used to think worshiping God was something we did on Sunday mornings, you know, just before the pastor speaks. But I've discovered that this just scratches the surface of worship. In reality, God invites us to ditch the other distractions and worship Him between the songs. Every day of the week.

A while back I was hanging out at a friend's

house. A group of us were chatting about summer plans and our upcoming road trips. Then a friend turned on the TV and a tasteless show came on. The conversation halted, and I felt convicted. *Should I say something?* I felt my heart pound as I weighed the reactions that might follow. *If I step out, people would call me a wimp, or holier-than-thou,* I thought. I was fighting an internal battle,

TODAY'S PLAYLIST

Jesus Lord of Heaven :: Phil Wickham
Beautiful Day :: Jamie Grace
My Adoration :: The Sonflowerz

whether to please people or honor God. I knew what we were watching was not enabling us to worship Him.

I had a choice to make. *Speak out!* was the urging my heart responded to. I went for it. Collecting everything within me to find a loving, humble way, I asked my friend if she would change the channel. Yeah, she wasn't thrilled.

But here's the conviction I had elected to live with, "A time will come, however, indeed it is already here, when the true (genuine) worshipers will worship the Father in spirit and in truth (reality); for the Father is seeking just such people as these as His worshipers" (John 4:23, Amplified Bible).

Bringing God authentic worship isn't easy when we have to go against the flow—the opposite way from what feels comfortable!

When have you ever felt this way? **Write down** a time when you were reluctant to go against what everyone else was doing but made a stand anyway.

DESCRIBE~

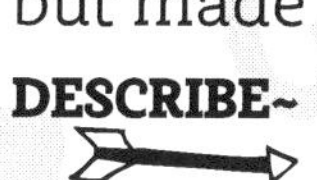

If you think about it, loving God and worshipping Him are tied together. Our thoughts and actions are the main avenue that all our love for God can funnel through. And it's His unconditional love for us that activates a response of worship from within.

Sooner or later you will be confronted with a choice. You'll be in a situation where you'll need to demonstrate courage if your words and actions are to reveal God. What will you choose?

Our hearts were not meant to worship temporary things. That Nissan Coupe will turn to rust someday. Popularity will come and go. That TV show will be outdated. I can't even compare those things to Jesus, who is always worthy of my worship, forever. This will never change! Then why do we choose to worship other things?

It isn't just the songs you sing that express worship to God. In the middle of the week, God is looking for your whole heart. Your attention. Your *response*. Today, let God's ever-present love for you be the fuel for your worship!

REFLECTION & ACTION

1. Write down **three** areas of your life where you desire to bring God worship. Given your unique circumstances, be specific about what it can look like.

1

2

3

2. Read Psalm 19:14. In your own words, ask God to help you live a life of devotion to Him no matter what.

3. What do you worship? For my friend, it's his car. What first comes to mind for you?

PSALM 86:9-10

in the limelight

MY HEAD WAS PRESSED against the window of the van as we drove into the slums of El Salvador. It was my first experience face-to-face with radical poverty. I had come with Compassion International to give supplies to the project churches and to hug my very own sponsor child. Stepping out of the van and into the alley, the sun's heat pounded down as unfamiliar, musty smells filled the air.

There in the alley I met Stephanie, an 18-year-old who had recently lost her mother in a tragic accident. Desperately trying to fix the leaky roof in a storm, her mother slipped and fell. Stephanie looked like someone who could have gone to school with me! Instead, she was raising her sisters and brothers by herself, with no running water, and a makeshift fireplace for a kitchen.

My heart sank. I forgot about the heat.

Where I come from, a day without electricity is a rare inconvenience (and a huge one, if I'm honest), but for Stephanie, pure water is hard to come by. I was compelled to reach out to her with the compassion of God in any way I could. But first, my heart had to change.

It was Jesus who began the revolution of compassion and love.

I will never live the same since the day I stepped off that plane in El Salvador. I saw so much hopelessness, pain, and dirt! I adopted a radically different view of what compassion looks like. God changed my heart from a me-focused view to a love-focused vision.

TODAY'S PLAYLIST

The Face of Jesus :: The Sonflowerz
Know Us By Our Love :: Moriah Peters
Build Your Kingdom Here :: Rend Collective Experiment

This transformation in me was inspired by the life of Jesus. He gave us a clear answer to what God thinks about suffering and difficulty in the world, like the kind I saw firsthand in El Salvador.

Flip through the pages of Matthew, Mark, Luke, and John and you will discover overwhelming accounts of Jesus's undeniable sympathy and compassion. What did He think about the multitudes of people who were hungry, broken, and diseased? "When Jesus landed and saw a large crowd, he had compassion on them and healed their sick" (Matthew 14:14).

When Jesus encountered two blind men on the side of the road, He "had compassion on them and touched their eyes" (Matthew 20:34). And even on the cross, bearing pain on our account, He saw His mother, Mary, and told His disciple to take care of her (John 19:25–27).

Even when I cannot see him, I can hear the beautiful gallop of God's heartbeat for humanity.
~Christine Caine

His concern for us is unending. As we go about our daily lives struggling through math tests, sleepless nights, or troubling friendships, Jesus is with the Father praying for us (Romans 8:34)!

Jesus knows our issues and through His loving grace He helps us overcome. He began the revolution of compassion and love! He engaged His heart in saving the lost and spent every ounce of His energy reaching out to others.

Now, what does mirroring the compassion of Jesus look like in our own backyards?

My mom used to complain that she never utilized her fancy bread machine enough. It sat on the counter, and I longed for that smell of fresh-bread-yumminess to

When the main ingredient is compassion, our actions can have a lasting effect.

fill the house! Finally, one day she cracked open the lid and began preparing the dough. I asked why, and I was surprised by her story.

Our neighbor two houses down had recently had the shock of her life when she found out that her husband had been raiding banks. She had no idea it was going on until the police came to take him to jail! Mom went to talk with our neighbor and came home carrying a heavy heart. Dusting off her bread machine, she went into high gear whipping up some love. It was her way of giving. Freshly baked, warm bread and a handful of CDs were delivered that evening.

Years later, after we had moved, I ran into that neighbor. The first thing she said was how much that loaf of bread meant to her. Apparently, when the main ingredient is compassion, our actions can have a lasting effect. Here is our chance to become the hands and feet of Jesus!

REFLECTION & ACTION

1. 1 Peter 3:8 reads, "Finally, all of you, be like-minded, be sympathetic, love one another, be compassionate and humble." What are **two** ways you can show compassion to those around you in a practical, tangible way?

1

2

2. How has God shown compassion to you lately?

SYM·PA·THY
[sim-puh-thee]
the power of sharing the feelings of another

PSALM 103:8
2 CORINTHIANS 1:3-4

my thoughts

in the limelight

let's GET together

MY MOM SURRENDERED HER LIFE to Jesus when she was twenty. While visiting a friend in Kansas City, she was introduced to real church. Here's what I mean by real: These midwestern Jesus freaks were sincere in their love for God and people, generous in their giving, and exuberant in their joy. My mom tells me she had never seen anything like it.

Growing up in England, her only exposure to religion had been singing a few hymns at her dull (and mandatory) boarding school chapels. Her first impression of "real church" in Kansas City was vastly different.

This British girl found a warm Midwest welcome when she decided to stay for a while. New friends at the church gave her a bed, some sheets, and even a job! The love of Jesus was so tangible through the believers that she was stirred to know God. Their kindness forever left an impression.

Everyone has a different opinion about church. For my mom, it was a life-changing experience, and living proof that church—the people, not the building!—is a good thing when it's done right.

Everyone has a different opinion about church.

What are three words that you could use to describe church?

-
-
-

In the Bible, the church is called the body of Christ. Jesus is the "Head" of the body. We are made one through Christ.

TODAY'S PLAYLIST

We Depend On You :: The Sonflowerz
The Lost Get Found :: Britt Nicole
Come Together :: Third Day

Think about it like this, "The way God designed our bodies is a model for understanding our lives together as a church: every part dependent on every other part" (1 Corinthians 12:25, The Message). When people of mixed ages, races, and backgrounds come together with love and devotion to Christ and each other, you've got church! The family of God. Lovely togetherness.

But somewhere along the way our culture has lured us into thinking that virtual communication like texting, instant messaging, and Facebook fulfills our need for relationships.

Even with other believers, these virtual rituals will never replace genuine face time. Don't you think the false

About two thirds of teens who attend church in high school STOP going once they graduate, according to Barna Group.

sense of community we get online causes us to disengage where it matters most? Yes, I do too. So don't let some kind of virtual black hole replace your "church family" time.

Heading into college, some of my friends abandoned going to church. They just didn't think it a worthy investment of their time, especially with a busy class schedule. Church can seem like an extra-curricular activity, but all over the world, believers in Christ risk their lives in order to meet together! Their freedom to worship God is often severely limited by government institutions.

Most of us live on safe soil, making it easy to take church for granted. Right?

Do you ever wonder what Heaven will be like? I suspect Heaven is really the most outrageous church service ever (and never boring)! Believers from every nation will worship together, and with our own eyes we will see our Savior (Revelation 7:9-10). Today, when church is done right, it can be our glimpse into Heaven.

When you think about your future, do you envision yourself taking root in a local church and serving there? Wherever you may go to college or move to one day, finding the perfect church isn't the point. Being an active part of the body of Christ is. Without a doubt, God is calling you to this. If the Church is a body, we need every part involved. Don't be the missing elbow or eye or hand that everyone is looking around trying to find!

I love flipping through the photo album of my mom's first year as a believer. And it's not just because the hippie hair and bell-bottoms make me laugh. I can see, in every picture, the way church is meant to be.

REFLECTION & ACTION

1. How do these ideas change your perspective on church?

2. Name **two** favorite things about your church.

1

2

3. Spend a minute asking God to show you how you can be involved in your church.

JE·SUS FREAK
[jee-zuh s freek]
1. a member of the Christian youth revival, a national movement that began in the late 1960s
2. a devout Christian

COLOSSIANS 3:16
HEBREWS 10:25

my thoughts

in the limelight

day 33

MADE TO SHINE

by elissa

JENNA PEEKED HER HEAD over the edge of a large concrete drainage ditch behind her house. "Jack! Get out of there!" she called. Her four-year-old brother had insatiable curiosity and Jenna was the one to chase him down this time. Jack slowly emerged and Jenna scooped him in her arms. "Next time I'm sending Dad after you," she said, squeezing him tight.

Walking back into her house with Jack by the hand, she could hear her parents' voices talking in the kitchen. The neighbor, Mrs. Murphy, was there too. "I'm afraid to lose everything," Mrs. Murphy said in a shaky voice. Jenna stopped by the front door, letting Jack loose to run inside. Her best friend was Brooke Murphy. *Lose everything? What does that mean?* Jenna thought.

She darted across the street and knocked on the door. Brooke met her there. "Are you okay?" Jenna asked. "Your mom sounds worried." Brooke stepped out to sit on the front step, her long brown hair pulled into a ponytail. "My dad lost his job

yesterday and they aren't taking it very well," Brooke confided and continued to explain the situation.

Jenna knew that God would be there for Brooke no matter what. But she wasn't sure Brooke knew it. Last week Jenna had read the scripture, "As I have loved you, so you must love one another. By this everyone will know

TODAY'S PLAYLIST

Radiate :: Trisha Brock
Made To Shine :: The Sonflowerz
The Difference :: Shine Bright Baby

that you are my disciples, if you love one another" (John 13:34–35). She wasn't sure how to love Brooke in that moment, except to listen and pray.

Could it be that this is what shining for God looks like on any given day?

This idea of shining isn't reserved for pastors or just for Sundays. It doesn't feel like a heroic act or any kind of major accomplishment. It's a lifestyle of knowing who you are—a daughter of God—and radiating His love to the world around you.

For Jenna, her shine came out when her friend was hurting and when her brother needed some extra attention. When does your shining come out?

This is how The Message paraphrase puts it: **"You're here to be light, bringing out the God-colors in the**

world. God is not a secret to be kept. We're going public with this, as public as a city on a hill. If I make you light-bearers, you don't think I'm going to hide you under a bucket, do you? I'm putting you on a light stand. Now that I've put you there on a hilltop, on a light stand—shine! Keep open house; be generous with your lives. By opening up to others, you'll prompt people to open up with God, this generous Father in heaven" (Matthew 5:14–16).

What I didn't tell you about Jenna is that she has a difficult learning disorder and a slight lisp. She's still waiting to get contacts to replace the scratched up glasses, and last week she dropped her entire lunch tray on the cafeteria floor. Then there are the classmates that have a constant flow of sarcastic comments and nicknames for her.

Shining doesn't feel like a heroic act or any kind of major accomplishment.

All of this should have the power to devastate her. Well, not Jenna. She knows a million times over that God treasures her. It's there in black and white throughout God's love letters. Jenna is *made* to shine.

Evil has one purpose: extinguish the light inside of us.

But God's brightest light, His very Spirit, lives inside Jenna eliminating the darkness that tries to crowd in from the outside.

Our song "Made To Shine" goes like this:

God's love is a fire inside of you,
No one can take that away
You were made to shine a brilliant light
To radiate His glory
More than the stars in the night sky
You were made to shine

Girls, as you close this book for the final time today, take a look out your window. See the sun or get a glance of the moon peaking from behind the clouds. Notice how immovable and constant it is. You have the capacity to shine brighter than these! Since God is for you, who can be against you?

Jenna is taking up a great challenge. And it's your turn now. How will you shine the God-colors of love and true life into your world?

REFLECTION & ACTION

1. Pray about this "**Made To Shine**" challenge. Where do you think God wants you to start shining His love? Take a minute to ask Him.

2. Visit our website, www.sonflowerz.com/madetoshine and share **YOUR** Made To Shine story! You'll be spreading the light and encouraging your sisters in Christ who are also reading this book!

SHINE
[shahyn]
to glow or be bright
with reflected light

1 JOHN 1:5-7
MATTHEW 5:14-16
PSALM 18:27-29

You've read the book, now what?

Take our Made To Shine Challenge! We're asking you to get creative, and with a beautiful boldness *live out* Matthew 5:14-16. How can you radiate God's love to the world around you?

Visit **www.Sonflowerz.com/madetoshine**

Share your recent SHINE story and it will encourage other girls to do the same!

- *Watch our video message to you & check out other SHINE stories*
- *Comment about your favorite DAY in the book & tell us why*
- *Or write to us: team@sonflowerz.com*

Write about an idea you have to make a difference for Christ! Maybe you want to start a bible study with some friends, or offer to help your mom cook this week, or maybe you've decided to speak up about your faith to someone who needs to know Jesus.

You are the light!
- Elissa & Becca

Connect

TWITTER www.twitter.com/sonflowerz
FACEBOOK www.facebook.com/sonflowerzofficial
YOUTUBE www.youtube.com/thesonflowerz
PINTEREST www.pinterest.com/thesonflowerz
INSTAGRAM www.instagram.com/sonflowerz

MADE TO SHINE

a girls only event with The Sonflowerz

We are passionate about being a bold voice for today's girls – through music, writing and speaking!

MADE TO SHINE girls only event is a night to equip 6th – 12th grade young women to shine boldly for God in every area of their lives.

Hang out with us, hear personal stories, a live concert and discover the massive love God has for us! Don't miss it!

Elissa

MADE TO SHINE

an event for moms and daughters
with The Sonflowerz

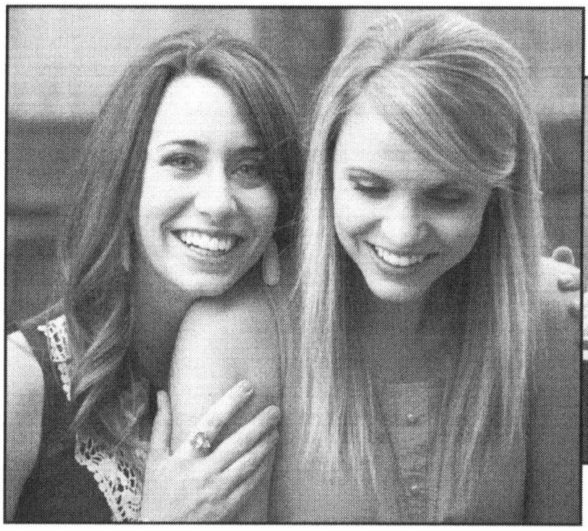

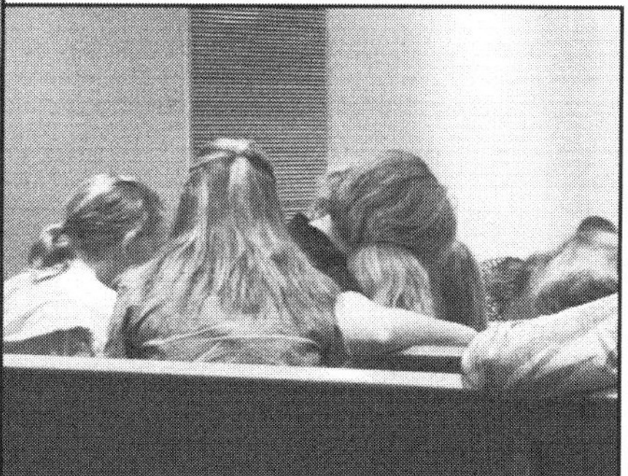

Focusing on relationship building, Made To Shine mother-daughter event includes a special speaker for the mothers, as well as an extra session where girls and moms join together in worship and in studying God's Word.

Host an Event Visit Sonflowerz.com Email Us Booking@Sonflowerz.com